Pyt. Programming for Beginners

The Ultimate Crash Course to Learn Python Computer Language Faster and Easier

Introduction to Machine Learning and Artificial Intelligence

By Dylan Mach

Table of content

Introduction

Congratulations on purchasing *Python programming for beginners: The ultimate crash course to learn python computer language faster and easier* and thank you for doing so.

In this book, you will find a lot of really important and essential theories that will help you to get started into the Python programming language. Besides, you will find a lot of examples that will help you to understand in a more visual way the things that we have explained here.

In the following chapters you will find a short introduction to how programming languages started, who invented Python, who uses python nowadays, and all the information that is needed to learn Python from scratch such as variables, operators, data types, functions, loops, statements, exceptions, how to create classes, modules, a whole chapter about Object-Oriented Programming, also known as OOP, file handling of .txt, .PDF, .xlsx, and a lot of information that will make you a Python programmer.

We strongly recommend reading the codes here written, analyze them, understand them, and then try to do an example using each one of them in order to remember them easily. Because as you will see, there are tons of commands and statements that won't be easy to learn and remember if they are not used

There are plenty of books on this subject on the market, thanks again for choosing this one! Every effort was made to ensure it is full of as much useful information as possible, please enjoy!

Chapter 1:
Introduction to Python

We can define programming as the process of designing, coding, debugging and maintaining the source code of a computer program, which means, that we say the steps to follow for the creation of the source code of computer programs.

The programming language, are all those rules or regulations, symbols and particular words used for the creation of a program, and with it, offer a solution to a particular problem. The best-known programming languages are: Basic (1964), C++ (1983), Python (1991), Java (1995), C# (2000), among others.

Programming is one of the stages for software development; programming specifies the structure and behavior of a program, verifying if it is working properly or not. Programming includes the specification of the algorithm defined as the sequence of steps and operations that the program must perform to solve a problem, for the algorithm to work, the program must be implemented in a compatible and correct language.

We could consider programming even easier than learning a new language because the programming language will be governed by a set of rules, which are, generally, always similar so you could say that it might be considered as a natural language.

In order to better understand the subject of programming, we could start with the beginnings of programming and how all this universe of languages and programs we know today began. We could start saying that programming began when the first computer was created in the fifteenth century, when a machine capable of doing basic operations and square roots appeared (Gottfried Wilhelm von Leibniz), although the one that actually served as a great influence for the creation of the first computer was the differential machine for calculating polynomials with the support of Lady Ada Countess (1815-1852), known as the first person who entered programming, and from whom comes the name of the programming language ADA, created by the DoD (Department of the United States), in the 1970s.

Initially, it was programmed in binary codes (bi=2), in other words, it consists of strings of 0s and 1s, which is the language directly understood by the computer, or what is known as machine language, a language considered fundamental for the commuter to be thus capable of interpreting the information supplied. Later the languages of high level appeared, using words in English, to give orders to follow, using intermediate processes between the language and the computer, this process can be a compiler or an interpreter.

The syntax of these programming languages is much simpler than our languages and they use a much smaller vocabulary and set of rules. In summary, we could say that programming is a set of sentences written in a programming language that tells the computer what tasks to perform and in what order, through a series of instructions that fully detail the process.

In the world of programming languages, we find interpreted languages, such as javascript, where a program called interpreter executes the sentences while reading the text file where they are written, which is why these programs are often also called scripts.

On the other hand, we have compiled languages such as Java, in this case, we must previously convert the text file to a "translation" through a program called compiler and the resulting file is the one that will finally run on the computer.

In this book we will speak specifically of the Python programming language, being this an interpreted language whose main and most important characteristic is the application of a syntax that favors the application of readable code. We could say that the interpreter is a type of program that executes a code directly, that is to say, it does not need to be compiled, and that is the case of our target language.

What is Python?

Python is one of the most important programming languages nowadays, being a general-purpose language, in this book you will have the language bases so that you can start with it. With this language, you can create a huge and variated amount of applications, because it allows you to create different kinds of applications since it doesn't have a defined purpose.

History of Python

This language was created by Guido Van Rossum in the early 1990s, at the Centre for Mathematics and Informatics (CWI, Netherlands), specifically in 1989, as Van Rossum himself explained in one of his interviews:

"In December 1989, I was looking for a hobby programming project to keep me busy during the Christmas weeks. My office would be closed and I would have nothing but my computer at home. I decided to write an interpreter for the new scripting language I had been coming up with recently: an ABC descendant that Unix/c hackers would like. I chose Python's name for the project, finding myself in a slightly irreverent state of mind (and being a big fan of Monty Python's Flying Circus)."

It began to be implemented in December 1989, and in February 1990 was released the first public version, version 0.9.0. Version 1.0 was released in January 1994, version 2.0 was released in October 2000 and version 3.0 was released on December 2008.

This programming language has as fundamental philosophy to have a syntax that favors a readable code, it is a high-level language that can be extended with C or C++, it has several programming environments that allow to edit programs, interact with the interpreter, develop projects, debug, among others and at the moment it is supported by a large community that facilitates its learning and that is producing a new progress in its already known new versions.

Python is a high-level programming language, interpreted and multipurpose, being currently one of the most used programming languages for software development. In recent years it has become a very valuable tool in the area of programming, this language is under a license of free software, under a license of Open Source or open-source approved by OSI (Open System Interconnect), so it is a program that can be used and distributed freely, either for personal or commercial use. The purpose of Python Software Foundation, "is to promote, protect and advance the Python programming language and to support and facilitate the growth of a diverse and international community of Python programmers".

The main advantage of an open and free technology is that it can be used without having to cover licensing costs. Free software is one of the most popular technological movements in the 21st century.

This language can be executed from any environment and distributed at the discretion of the user, modify if necessary, thus having a quick and easy basic tool for building programs.

To understand why we must learn python, it is necessary to understand the main characteristics of this language, that is why we will start talking about its main characteristics:

- It is a multiparadigm programming language, which means that we do not have to focus on a single way of programming, but we can do object-oriented programming, iterative programming, and functional programming, so we are not forced to focus on a single paradigm, hence its name of multiparadigm.

• It is a multiplatform language, which indicates that we can program in different environments or operating systems, such as Windows, Linux, etc..

• It is a very easy language to learn because it is simple and minimalist, and this is one of the main reasons why most people decide to have Python as their first programming language, because it has the simplest syntax to learn, it is an interpreted language, by this we mean that when executing a program, it will have the ability to execute itself taking instruction by instruction.

• It uses a dynamic typed, that can be explained in the following way, when we create a variable, and we store an initial type of data to it, the dynamic typed means that throughout the program this variable could change and store another value of another type of data, that later we will see this in detail.

• At the moment, we can also point out that this language occupies the position number four of the TIOBE index, which is an index that catalogs the languages according to their current popularity, being Java in first place, then in second place is the C language, in the third place is the C++ language and in the fourth Python, which indicates that it is a very popular and widely used language nowadays.

Now, knowing the characteristics of the program it is important to differentiate why we should learn Python and how it will serve us, what we can program with it, so well, being a general-purpose language, almost everything can be programmed with it: such as desktop applications with graphical interfaces and databases, web applications, games, custom applications, as a point of sale system for your business, for example, artificial intelligence, among others.

We will now talk about the development environment of this language, we can say that a development environment is a text editor in which we will be able to copy all the Python code, run our programs, do our tests, and so on. We will mention some of these editors, such as PyCharm, PyDev, Sublime Text 3, ATOM, VIM, as well as many others, in this book we will work with Visual Studio Code.

What can I do with Python?

As it is an easy to learn language, meaning it has a quite high learning curve, like many modern languages, as well as a very clean and simple syntax, as explained above, it is a very versatile language, because with it and the standard library we can write desktop applications and web applications. Python has excellent support for object-oriented programming (OOP), the only limitation for this language is your imagination. This programming language is built in such a way that there will always be a more optimal way to do things. This language is also used to work with artificial intelligence or robotics, where it is currently most used is for Big Data as it is a language that can handle a lot of data and complex operations.

In the area of video games:

The area of video games has its advantages and disadvantages, being Python an interpreted language, it is twice (or more) slower than a compiled language like Java, C++ or C#; you can do wonders of games in Python using libraries such as Pygame, SDL2 (Binding), OpenGL (binding), only that your game will not run as an executable made with C++ for example, instead it will run with the Python interpreter. But you will have an excellent language with a lot of support and documentation, and very few lines of code.

Finally, we can mention the scientific area, this is where Python shines. The syntax of Python and the bunch of libraries it gives you by default makes it perfect for scientific programming, plus in the Python community, there are huge libraries for mathematics and all that this entails.

Why should we use Python as a programming language?

Mainly we could say that we should use it because it is a very versatile language and general-purpose, this means that if your scope is not defined, you can create a huge number of applications using this language, suppose that your main goal is to create a web application, with Python you can do it, but probably tomorrow your interest will focus on scientific applications, because with Python you can also do it. In fact, the main development area of this language is the scientific area, if on the opposite you want to develop a low-level application, or you would like to use it in hardware because it is also possible to do it with this programming language, it is absolutely possible. That is why we talk about it being a versatile language since it does not have a rigorously defined scope.

Who uses Python today?

At the present time, this programming language is very commonly used, in addition, it has a wide range of uses, from the compilation and processing of data to the learning of a computer, which is why many of the important companies are currently working with this versatile programming language. We will mention some of these companies:

1. Google; it is a company that has handled this language from practically its beginning, in fact, its founders explained in one of their interviews that, "Python where we can, C++ where we

must". This leads us to think that C++ is used for Google when memory control is imperative. So it is currently one of the company's official languages along with C++, Java and Go, which are the other three languages used. It is worth mentioning that Guido van Rossum himself worked in Google from 2005 to 2012, which indicates how important Python is for Google.

2. Facebook; in this company, Python is also part of this important social network, being in third place of language most used just behind C++, for example; in this company are handled more than five thousand confirmations of service and utilities such as infrastructure management, binary distribution, hardware images, and operational automation. As we have mentioned before, the ease of use of Python's libraries helps engineers to avoid having to maintain so many codes, making it easier to focus on brand optimization.

3. Spotify; one of the most important music companies today, is a large Python operator, due to how fast it is to write and encode on it. To provide suggestions and recommendations for all its users, Spotify relies heavily on a large volume of analysis and has Luigi, which is a Python module that synchronizes with Hadoop.

4. Netflix; this company uses python in a similar way to Spotify as it relies on this language to enhance its server-side analysis. Most of the engineers who work for this company are free to choose the language to work with, and most of them choose this language to encode.

5. Dropbox; this cloud-based storage system uses this language in its client's desktop. In 2012 Rossum joined this company on the condition that they would allow him to be just an engineer, not a leader or a manager, during his time at the company he helped to generate the ability to share data warehouses with other users within the Dropbox community.

6. Industrial Light and Magic (ILM) is a special effects center, founded by George Lucas himself in 1975, to create special effects for the well-known movies Star Wars. ILM selected Python 1.4, because it is much faster to integrate into their existing infrastructure, also, the easy Interoperability of Python with C+ and C++ made easy for ILM to import Python into their patented lighting software.

In this way we can see how Python is in more and more places, using this language to wrap software components, expand graphic applications, among other skills, it has a wide range of code libraries and is more sensitive in development areas

How do I know which Python version should I use?

In Python, there are currently two versions that are incompatible between themselves, which causes a lot of confusion to any user who is starting to program or even any user who is starting in the same language. These versions are called Python 2.x which was released in 2000 and was updated until 2010, however, in 2008 was released version 3.x which is currently in full development of new versions and improvements in their commands.

But, do these versions contain the same tools?

Well, there is a big difference between each version of Python among which highlights that in Python 3.x the print sentence is taken into account as a function, so it is necessary to call it and enclose in parentheses what you want to print. Unlike in the version 2.x which does not need parentheses to print.

When you are going to iterate a dictionary in Python version 2.x, the key-value elements are used through the items() and iteritems() methods. In the current version of Python 3.x, this operation is done only through the items(), keys() and values() methods and when using the iteritems() method we will obtain an exception of the AttributeError type.

There is also a change in the input function, which in the Python 2.x version takes the data without converting the variable type. In this version, if we enter an integer variable, its entry will be of the "int" type and if we want it to be treated as a string we would have to call the function "raw_input" since this will be in charge of converting "int" data to string.

In the Python 3.x version, this takes a big step forward since the "raw_input" function is suppressed and any conversion would be easily done through the input() function.

Now that I know which version to use, how can I install Python according to my operating system?

The Python programming language is included by default in the Mac OS and Linux operating systems, the only thing to do is to update according to the version you have, however, for Windows users, the program must be installed since it is not included in the system.

Install Python on Windows
Go to https://www.python.org/downloads/

Choose the version of your preference to install: 2.x and 3.x. It is always recommended for new users to use the latest version of Python (3.x), this facilitates understanding thanks to its simplified tools. However, if you are using a recycled code, it is recommended to use the version in which it was written.

Once the download is finished, run the program.
If you are a new user, it is recommended to install Python with its default settings. If you are a language experienced user, you can do the custom installation.

Verify that the program and its interpreter work correctly.

Install or upgrade Python for Mac OS

Python comes by default in OS X with version 2.7. If you need to upgrade your version to 3.x just follow these steps:

Enter python.org/downloads on your computer, the link will automatically detect the operating system you have and it will show you the files compatible with the computer to start the download.

Click on the PKG file to start its installation and if you are a new user.

Start the Python program by typing "Python3" in order to start the interface of this new version.

Installing or Upgrading Python For Linux

In almost all Linux distributions Python is previously installed by default, so it is not necessarily needed to install but rather update, the only detail is that for a policy issue of installation the vast majority comes with Python 2.x and not with Python 3.x, as should be, especially if we consider that most modern applications require or recommend version 3.x to compile. To upgrade Python, just follow these steps:

Check the Python version you have, since the Linux Operating System is included with the program, however, its version may vary.

On the Linux terminal type "sudoapt-get install Python".

Then in the same terminal type "sudo yum install Python".

Enter as a root user by typing "pacman-S python".

Finally, start the program and check that it works correctly so you can start programming.

Learning to use Python

Once Python is downloaded, you will need a code editor that allows you to interpret and write code for programs. There is a great variety of editors, this depends and goes according to the preference and level of experience of the user with the programming since it will be your ally while programming.

Among the best-known editors are:

Visual Studio Code: It is a multi-platform source code editor with a dark interface; it has an optimized user interface. This editor has multiple tools and even allows real-time updates of our code while compiling. You do not need a complete IDE and it is possible to change the appearance of your interface through the themes it brings.
Visual Studio Code supports a wide variety of languages, including Python, Php, Java, C++, Ruby, Go, C, SQL, JavaScript, Batch, and Objective-C.

Sublime text: This is a multiplatform editor with a dark interface, which allows to execute a great variety of documents in multiple tabs and offers a full-screen mode, thus facilitating the user's visual space in the computer. This has a panel that allows you to move through the code quickly and easily. Sublime text is capable of interpreting a wide variety of programming languages such as Python, CSS, C++, HTML, Matlab, R, SQL, C, Php) and has autosave, another fact and advantage of this editor is that it allows running files in Python with just a shortcut on the keyboard; Ctrl+B.

Geany: This is a multiplatform code editor of the Linux operating system, which is ideal for application development and even software development for this operating system and also that it is possible to operate on operating systems such as Windows, Mac OS or any other system with GTK library support. In addition, this editor is distinguished for being fast and lightweight, is completely independent and supports languages such as HTML, C++, JAVA, PHP, PYTHON, and C.

Wing: This is another paid integrated development environment for Python, it is owned by the company Wingware. It was created mainly for professional developers. It offers a great set of tools and features necessary for Python programming, it is compatible with Windows, OS X, and Linux and works with Python 3.x versions. Wing has a free basic version, a personal edition and a professional edition which can be considered very powerful when creating a program.

Komodo Edit: This is an open-source editor oriented to dynamic languages including Python, JavaScript, HTML, CSS, Perl, NodeJS. Komodo is considered one of the most popular code editors for applications today and also has a premium package that includes a number of useful tools, such as allowing writing codes and collaborating in the development of other codes in real-time, exploring databases, removing bugs. It is mostly focused on small project developers.

Ninja IDE: This is a text editor for development, which will only allow us to create projects in Python and at the same time run them in order to correct any errors that may occur at any moment.

Python's Keywords:

It is well known that in every programming language there is a series of words and commands which are found in a reserved way and can not be used for anything other than to fulfill its function. In Python there is also has a set of words, these are called: reserved words or keywords, and are nothing more than a set of words in which each element contains a special meaning and is an indispensable part of the syntax of its language for the correct development of the code.

These words must be written exactly as shown in the following table, which will contain some of the reserved words of the language. If this is not done, the program will not be able to recognize them and can generate a type of exception called: NameError, this is because Python does not distinguish between upper and lower case or as it is formally known: case sensitive.

If we write false, the Python interpreter will not be able to understand that we are referring to the False operator and will throw us an error because this is not defined.

The following table will show the set of keywords for the Python 3.x version (version with which we are going to work in the next programs), which have defined approximately 33 reserved words; these same ones form the nucleus of the syntax of this programming language.

"and"	"def"	"finally"	"in"	"or"	"while"
"as"	"del"	"for"	"is"	"pass"	"with"
"assert"	"elif"	"from"	"lambda"	"raise"	"yield"
"break"	"else"	"global"	"None"	"return"	
"class"	"except"	"if"	"nonlocal"	"True"	
"continue"	"False"	"import"	"not"	"try"	

Of this group, there are a certain number of words which are considered " essential ", these could be the ones we are going to use the most and we will explain them in-depth in the next chapters.

True & False: These expressions are those whose values are thrown to us by the program as a result of evaluating logical expressions.
and & or: These expressions are those that we use as connectors for the logical expressions (True & False), in order to be able to create much more complex expressions.

if, elif & else: These expressions are those which are used to build blocks of conditions, in order to make certain decisions within the same programs.

For & while: These expressions are used to build loops or formally: repetitive blocks.

Def & return: These expressions are those that represent instructions, which will be used to define our own functions. In other words: these expressions represent a series of instructions that will be in charge of carrying out a certain task as indicated.

Import & from: These expressions are those used to add additional functionalities.

If you are using a code that has been written in Python 2.x version or you simply want to start in this version, we can see that unlike Python 3.x version, this version has only 31 reserved words or keywords.

"and"	"def"	"finally"	"in"	"print"	"yield"
"as"	"del"	"for"	"is"	"raise"	
"assert"	"elif"	"from"	"lambda"	"return"	
"break"	"else"	"global"	"not"	"try"	
"class"	"except"	"if"	"or"	"while"	
"continue"	"exec"	"import"	"pass"	"with"	

What are the differences in keywords between Python 2.x and Python 3.x?

Below, we will mention those important differences that cannot be noticed at first sight:

- Python 3.x incorporates the words "True", "False" and "None".

- In Python 2.x the words "exec" and "print" that were part of the keywords, become integrated functions in Python 3.x with the syntax exec() and print().

How can I find these words?

In Python, there is a module whose name is known as keyword module of the standard library, this is responsible for exporting a list called: kwlist. which contains all the keywords that are reserved in our programming language, Python.

Another easier way to consult these keywords is through the help() command, this is just a function that comes integrated and facilitates us to consult information, documentation and get a clearer help on the components of our program.

If in any given situation you need to quickly consult the operation or meaning of a particular keyword (only of the Python programming language), you can do it through the command help(), once introduced this, you must write the keyword to consult and immediately will show us on screen all the information of the word requested.

Python syntax and its importance

Now we will talk about the most important thing and it will be what will allow us to advance in our code and in programming in general: The syntax; we know very well that Python is an interpreted programming language, but what does this really mean?

Our Python programming language works through tabulations, this is informally known as indentation or spaces. This means that, at the moment of executing a program, it is going to follow an order of interpretation, which works through the tab key on our keyboard which is just the key containing arrows located above Caps Lock, these tabs work in each loop or conditional sentence.

When we have a correct indentation we can avoid the use of keys and brackets and we can even avoid some reserved words to start and end a program that marks a block of code. This allows the program to have better use and operation.

Having a good indentation also helps us to make our code look uniform in order to facilitate reading and provide comfort to any third party who reads it, and even to ourselves, because we can locate an error effectively and quickly.

It is important to emphasize that the first line of the code should never be indented, the indentation will always go after this and with 4 boxes of space.

Physical and logical lines: A program in Python is composed of a set of logical lines, they are formed by a certain amount of physical lines.
But... What are physical lines?

Physical lines are those lines that are used to enumerate our code editor, or formally can be described as a sequence of characters which end when entering the end-of-line character "\n".

And what are logical lines?

Logical lines are those that go with Python syntax logic components and their end is determined by the NEWLINE token which determines the end of each line and starts another.

These physical lines have the ability to be united through an action called "implicit union of lines" to form a single logical line, using characters such as parentheses (), square brackets [] and keys {}.

If we start a logical line with the start characters such as "(", "[", "{" it will extend through all the necessary logical lines until it ends with its closing symbol ")", "[", "{".

There are two types of statements in Python:

Simple statements: These types of statements are those that must be completed in a single logical line. For example:

Print objects in the program: print()

Generate exceptions: raise EndSearch (location)

Access Attributes: from sys import stdin

Access modules: import sys

Execute functions through expressions: log.write()

Compound statements: These types of statements are those that must begin with the compound statement clause, followed by the contained statement on the next line. This must be correctly indented since it will be part of the body of our code. It will always start with a keyword and end with a colon ":".

An example of compound sentences is sequence and iteration for, else, else, if, elif, loops while, and else.

Make comments in the code: A comment in Python refers to a set of characters which are not executable, these are made in a text line of our program. The comment is represented with the numeral character (#). At the moment of programming, the comments can be very useful to be able to explain in detail each action carried out in a program code to people outside the code, or even for ourselves.

Our first program: Hello world

Once we have installed the code editor of our preference and already knowing a little about the Python programming language syntax, we can proceed to write our first program: Hello world.

If you already have experience in programming is common to ask yourself, "Why is "Hello World" always the first program to enter any programming language? Well, the simple phrase Hello World is characterized by being an extremely simple code, especially at the time of running and can serve as a test to ensure that we have installed our program well and its interpreter. In this way, when working with heavy programs we are going to be sure that everything will work correctly. From now on all the examples will be based on version 3.x for better understanding.

The syntax that we are going to use for this code will be: print("Hello World");

Running a program on Linux

1. Create a directory called projects on your primary user's desktop
2. Create a plain text file with the name: Helloworld.py
3. Type the syntax of your code
4. Run the following command: Home/projects/Helloworld.py.
5. Once this is done, your code should be displayed as indicated.

To run in windows:

1. Create a directory called projects in unit C: \
2. Within this directory, we'll need to create a plain text file
3. Write the code syntax
4. Save the file as Helloworld.py (the name may vary according to your preference)
5. Run from the MS-DOS console: C:Python27\Python C:\Projects\Helloworld.py, or also from the same program Visual Studio, you can do F5.
6. Once this is done, your code should be shown on screen as indicated.

Running a program on Mac OsX

1. Click on File in a new browser window.

2. Create a folder with the name of your preference, in which you will save future projects.

3. Within this folder, we will need to create a new folder called Projects (all programs will be stored here).

4. Click on Applications and then on TextEdit.

5. Select Plain Text.

6. Type the syntax of the program.

7. Click on "save as" from the menu file in TextEdit.

8. Save the file as: Helloworld.py (or the name of your preference) and select the folder already mentioned.

9. Select Applications, then utilities and terminal.

10. Select the folder in which you saved your program.

11. Run cd of the folder.

12. Execute ls and it should show on screen the file Helloworld.py

13. Type the following command: Helloworld.py

Once this is done, your code should be displayed as indicated

Chapter 2:
Variables

Flow control

What are flow diagrams?

They are tools that are used for any type of programming language, which are used to represent or create the structure of the program or algorithm.

The flow diagrams or also called flowchart, are a way to graphically represent an algorithm (the steps that are executed in the program), facilitating its interpretation to a person.

The creation of the structure of the algorithm or program can be considered the first part of the development of the algorithm and the preparation for the most important step that is coding.

At the time of elaborating a program, it is advisable to make a flowchart so that any person can understand in a simple way the function of the algorithm. Currently, there are a variety of software and online tools that facilitate the elaboration of these diagrams.

Main figures and meaning:

	Start / end: Indicates the starting or ending of the diagram
	Input / Output of data: These are data which are assigned to the input and output variables at the beginning and ending of our code.
	Process: This is what executes the order of the operation
	Decision: Indicates a position in the flowchart, this is used for logical expressions. In this case, the sequence is going to split in two cases, a positive and a negative one. This is also used to apply conditionals
	Document: This is used generally to make a document
	Inspection: This is used for some cases where an inspection is required.
	Flowline: This is used to indicate the direction of the diagram

For example:

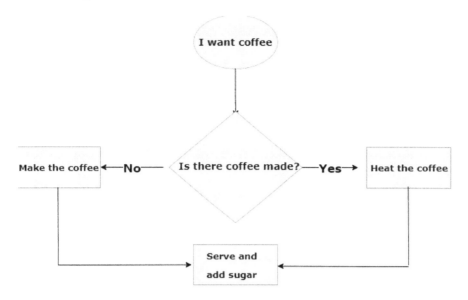

Variables

What are the variables in Python?

It is quite sure that we have always heard the concept of variable in mathematics since these are defined as an unknown symbol represented by letters (x, y, z, i, n) which (mostly) store a numerical value.

In this case, when we talk about variables in programming, these represent a space reserved in the memory of our program or computer that can be modified and used multiple times. These variables have a very similar representation and meaning; since they represent a box capable of storing values. Unlike mathematical variables, these can store complex words such as cities, names, passes, simple letters, and ages.

In Python, a variable can be interpreted as a "label" to the data information stored box, and these data can be understood as objects. Python is also able to distinguish between upper and lower case letters (as we previously mentioned this is known as case sensitive), which means that it will not be the same to call a variable Song to a variable called song.

We cannot forget that being Python a programming language that is object-oriented, the data structure of our programs will be based on these same, therefore, the label we put to the variables cannot match the names of the commands or otherwise it will throw us an error.

Declare variables in Python

Python has the advantage of being a dynamic programming language; this means that it is not necessary to specify the type of data with which we will work since its interpreter is able to infer the type of data to use. Unlike C++ that, to declare a variable, it is necessary and obligatory to specify the type of data with which the variable will be stored in the memory so that its compiler can be able to interpret it.

For example:

```
variable.py  ●

        ▷  variable.py
1       variable name= value
2
3
4
```

As we can see, Python uses the symbol "=" to assign the values to the variable, once this is done the variable starts with this value, since there is no possible way to declare a variable without any initial value.

```
variable.py  ●

▷ ...        ▷  variable.py ▷ ...
1    x= 2
2    X= 4
3
4
```

We can observe in this example the declaration of two variables of name x with different values, this is totally valid since as we can observe, a variable is written in small letters and another variable is written in capital letters.

It is important to keep in mind that in Python there are operations that, when defined, are not allowed between types (classes) that are not compatible, so that when each data is identified it becomes an inherited object to the type of data to which it belongs.

To be able to declare a variable it is necessary for it to go from left to right, otherwise, it will result in a syntax error.

28

```
variable.py ●
        ▷  variable.py
   1    2 = x
   2    4 = X
   3
   4       SyntaxError: can't assign to literal
```

It is essential that variable names begin with a letter or underscore (the rest of the name can contain letters, numbers, and underscores).

```
variable.py ●
        ▷  variable.py ▷ ...
   1    X= 2 # Valid #
   2    _X= 4 #Valid#
   3
   4    2x = 4 #Error, starts with numeral data #

           SyntaxError: invalid syntax

        !x = False # Error, starts with symbol #
           SyntaxError: invalid syntax
```

It is also possible to assign multiple values to multiple variables on the same line, as long as there are the same number of arguments on both the left and right.

```
        ▷  variable.py ▷ ...
   1    a, b, c= 2, 4, 6
   2
```

Data Types

- Integers: Integer data in Python can identify integers of either decimal, binary, hexadecimal, or octal type.

There are two ways to declare a variable as integer: An int is placed prior to the variable name as follows:

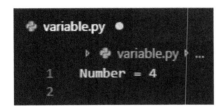

The other way is the most common, in which we only write the name of the variable to be declared.

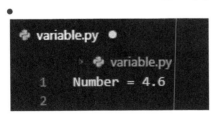

- Float: The data of the type float are in charge of covering all the set of real numbers ex: 3.14, 21, -85.6. When we perform an operation with float type data, it will not always give us a result with an exact number, many times it can be an approximation and its declaration is very similar to the declaration of variables of the integer type.

-

```
variable.py ●
        variable.py
1    Number = 4.6
2
```

- Complex: The data of the complex type refer to the set of operations with complex numbers, these are expressed as data of the type float separated by the operand symbol, the first number is going to present to the real number and its imaginary component is going to be identified being accompanied by a letter j. At the moment of declaring a variable of the complex type it must be declared in the following way:

●

```
variable.py ●
        variable.py ▶ ...
1    vari = complex(4+14j)
2    print(vari)
3
```

●   String: Data of the string type refers to a sequence or string of characters that are enclosed in apostrophes or quotation marks.

String types:

\": double quotation mark.

\': single quotation mark.

\n: Line break.

\t: Tab horizontally.

Example:

```
variable.py ●
        variable.py ▶ ...
1    string= "Hello world"
2    string2= "This is my String example"
3    print(string)
4    print(string2)
```

●   Bool: Boolean data consists of only two (2) digits, which evaluate logical expressions. This is very important for future chapters because it will allow us to understand conditionals or cycles.

If a logical expression is true, its numerical value will be 1.

If a logical expression is false, its numerical value will be 0.

• Lists: List type data allows the program to store within it, certain items of any different data type, as well as being able to have repeated items. These same are written with curly brackets.

•

```
variable.py ●

        variable.py ▸ ...
1    a = 2
2    b = 4
3    string = "Hello people"
4    bool= True
5
6    list=[a, b, string, bool, 3, False, "good luck"]
7
8    print(list)
```

• Tuples: Tuples type data are able to store several items within it, this type of data can be similar to lists but differs in the following things: Their declaration is made with a parenthesis (), unlike the lists that are declared with square brackets []; when we declare Tuples, these same are immutable, unlike the lists that when we declare them, can be changed, and finally because they are immutable, their search for data is much more effective than in a list.

His statement is as follows:

```
variable.py ●

    variable.py  ...
1   a = 2
2   b = 4
3   string = "Tuple"
4   bool= True
5
6   Tup=(a, b, string, bool)
7
8   print(Tup)
```

- Set: This type of data in Python is based on a data structure, which can consist of multiple elements whose order in the set is not defined. Sets are able to add, remove and iterate elements of a set, as well as perform common operations such as differentiate, verify if an element belongs to the set, differentiate and intersect.

To define a set we only need to name the function set (). If it has a list, a tuple or a string, it will return a compound of the elements. Example:

```
variable.py ✗

    variable.py  ...
1   A = {5, 3, 2}
2   A = set('PYTHON')
3   print(A)
```

- Dictionaries: This type of data is defined as a structure that has certain special characteristics that allow us to store any integer value, list, string, and even functions. Dictionaries allow us to identify each element by a key.

33

It is important to keep in mind that when working with dictionaries the 'keys' cannot be repeated data, likewise, it is not possible to access the keys through their associated value. It is also important to know that these do not meet a specific order, but that this type of data is guided by the keys.

In order to define a dictionary, we enclose with curly brackets {} the list of values to be entered. Each key pair is separated with commas and the key together with the value is separated by a colon. For example:

```
variable.py
    variable.py
1   user = {'name' : 'John', 'Age' : 20, 'Knowledge': ['Python progamming','C++ programming','JavaScript']}
2
3   print (user['name'])
4   print (user['Age'])
5   print (user['Knowledge'])
```

That will print:

```
John
20
['Python progamming', 'C++ programming', 'JavaScript']
```

Here we can see that we have created the dictionary and also the program shows us that we have accessed each key separately.

Dictionary methods:

get(): This method receives a key as a parameter and returns its value. If it doesn't find a value, it returns an object of type none. For example:

```
variable.py
    variable.py
1   user={'name' : 'John', 'age' : 20, 'knowledge': ['Python programming','C++ programming','JavaScript'] }
2   print(user.get('name'))
3
```

In this case, it will return the value name, which in this case will be John.

Item(): This type of method is in charge of returning a list of tuples, in which each one is composed of two elements in which the first element will be the key and the second element will be its value. For example:

```
variable.py ×
    variable.py ▸ ...
1   user={'name' : 'John', 'age' : 20, 'knowledge': ['Python programming','C++ programming','JavaScript'] }
2   print(user.items())
```

Keys(): This type of method only returns the keys of our dictionary. Example:

```
variable.py ×
    variable.py ▸ ...
1   user={'name' : 'John', 'age' : 20, 'knowledge': ['Python programming','C++ programming','JavaScript'] }
2   print(user.keys())
```

Values(): This type of method only returns the values of their respective keys from our dictionary.

```
variable.py ×
    variable.py ▸ ...
1   user={'name' : 'John', 'age' : 20, 'knowledge': ['Python programming','C++ programming','JavaScript'] }
2   print(user.values())
```

Clear(): This method eliminates all the items and leaves our dictionary empty. For example:

```
variable.py ×
    variable.py ▸ ...
1   user={'name' : 'John', 'age' : 20, 'knowledge': ['Python programming','C++ programming','JavaScript'] }
2   print(user.clear())
```

Copy(): This method returns a copy of the original dictionary. For example:

```
variable.py ×
    variable.py ▸ ...
1   user={'name' : 'John', 'age' : 20, 'knowledge': ['Python programming','C++ programming','JavaScript'] }
2   print(user.copy())
```

Redeclaring variables in Python:

A great advantage that Python has is its ability to allow redeclaring variables in a simple way, from changing their value to changing the type of variable without complications. For example:

```
variable.py

      variable.py  ...
1    a=4
2    print(a)
3    a=8
4    print(a)
5    a=True
6    print(a)
7    a= "Julia"
8    print(a)
9
```

In the last example, we can observe that the first declaration of the variable "a" is assigned the value 4, which is an integer, then the variable is redeclared with the value 8, therefore, at that time the variable is integer, then we have redeclared the variable again and we have converted it to a Boolean value, since we have assigned it the value True. Finally, we have assigned to the variable a string which we can see as a name "Julia" so at that time the variable is of string type.

Concatenate strings

To concatenate character strings we will only need to use the addition operand (+). It is important to note that you must specifically and explicitly mark the place where we want to leave the space blank.

```
variable.py ●

     ▷  variable.py ▷ ...
1    a= "Hello world"
2    b=" this is an example"
3    c= a + b
4    print(c)
```

As we can see in the last example, the variable "a" was created, which contained the value "Hello world", then the variable "b" was created, which contained the value "this is an example" and later the final variable "c" was created, this last one was in charge of carrying out the concatenation of "a" and "b".

The concatenation of variables can also be done with integer and boolean values, but to do this you must convert these variables into strings beforehand. How do you do this? Well, it's very simple, we do it calling the function str(). For example:

```
variable.py ✕

     ▷  variable.py ▷ ...
1    string= "class of "
2    date= 2019
3    date=str(date)
4    final=string + date
5    print(final)
```

As we could see in the example, we have created a string variable that contains the value "class of ", and then the integer type date variable is created and contains the value "2019". Then we redeclare our variable date to string type with the function str().

Another very common example is concatenating lists, this we do through the function extend(), for example:

```python
# variable.py
   # variable.py ...
1    lunch = ["Sanwich", "pizza", "Burger", "meat"]
2    snack = ["ice cream", "cookie", "brownie", "cake"]
3    lunch.extend(snack)
4    print(lunch)
```

We can see in the previous example that a list has been created with some lunch options; then another list has been created with some snack options and finally, the command lunch.extend(snack) is created concatenating list number 1 with list number 2.

Global Variables

Global variables are those used throughout the program; once declared, they may be used as a main function or any other type of function.

This type of variable can be modified in any part of the program, this could seem an advantage, but it could also cause confusion both for the programmer or another external person who is going to read the program. Another point that could be considered negative with global variables is that they can take up more space than common ones because they cannot be destroyed at the end of running the function, on the other hand, this one does not allow the code to be reusable; this makes Python programming language one of the most attractive.

In general terms, it is considered a bad practice to work with global variables, but it is never too much to have complete knowledge. Next, we will see how to declare a global variable. For this it is necessary to use the global command:

38

```
variable.py ●

        variable.py ▸ ...
1    global var
2    var = 2019
3    print(var)
```

As we could see in the last example, calling or declaring a global variable is not very complicated. We could say that it is similar to what we have seen to declare variables; the only difference is that from now on the variable "var" is going to have a global character so that any function is going to be able to access it in a simple way.

Local variables

Local variables are those that are only used in one function and are deleted from memory when their execution is completed. Unlike global variables, local variables allow us to save quantities of lines of codes, making modular programming much more agile and easy, thus allowing the reuse of the code, which makes Python one of the most striking programming languages.

The main advantage of using local variables in a Python program is that it facilitates the reading of the code, making it simple to understand; global variables allow any error to be fixed more effectively and easily. Having reduced lines of code, it is very unlikely that confusion will be generated at the time of interpreting it.

It is considered a good practice to use local variables at the moment of programming since nowadays it is intended to obtain much simpler codes to interpret by users who do not have so much experience in programming.

To better understand this, we will make an example that explains in a clear way the use of these variables at the moment of programming.

Example: We are going to create a problem in which it must be responsible for taking the following data from a person:

1. Name and Lastname
2. Age
3. Country of origin

```
variable.py ×
    variable.py ▸ ...
1   full_name = input("Full name: ")
2   age = input("Age: ")
3   country_origin = input("country of origin: ")
4   print("Full name"+full_name + "\n" + "Age"+ age + "\n"+"Country of origin" + country_origin)
5
```

We can observe that the syntax focuses more than everything on the input() command, what does this mean? This is only the function that allows a user-program interaction to be possible. In this way, the variables "full_name", "age" and "country_origin" will have the value that the user introduces at the moment to the console.

```
Full name: Python programmer
Age: 100
country of origin: Worldwide
```

Chapter 3: Operators

Operators are mathematical symbols that carry out a specific operation between operands, operators can receive variable operands. Operands are those arguments that operators receive in order to perform their functions. So we can conclude that operators are those special symbols that are capable of performing logical and arithmetic operations.

Types of operators:

- Logic operators.

- Arithmetic operators.

- Comparison operators.

- Assignment operators.

- Special operators.

• Logical or conditional operators: This type of operators are those that are commonly used to group, deny and exclude some expressions of our code.

1. Operator not: This type of operator is the one in charge of negating or returning a value opposite to the Boolean value.

not True=False.

not False=True.

2. Operator Or: This type of operator is the one that evaluates the values on the right side and the

values on the left side in order to finally return a true value if at least one condition is met.

False or True = True

True or false = True

True or True = True

False or False = False

3.   Operator And: This type of operator is responsible for assessing whether the conditions between the value on the left side and the value on the right side are met correctly:

True and False = False

True and True = True

False and True = False

False and False = False

•   Comparison operators: These types of operators are those that we use to compare (as its name says) some values stored in the program so that later this at the time of compiling we can return a value of the True / False type as a result of fulfilling a condition.

1.   Operator !=: This type of operator is in charge of evaluating if these stored values are different and depending on the result of the analysis, this will give us a True/False. E.g.

20!=20 The result is going to be False

14!= 15 The result will be True

2.　　Operator ==: This type of operator is in charge of evaluating if these values are the same for different types of data and depending on the result obtained in its analysis, its result will give us a True/False. E.g.

19 = = 19 The result will be True

10 = = 5 The result will be False

3.　　Operator >: This type of operator is in charge of evaluating whether the value entered on the left side has a position greater than that of the value positioned on the right side. E.g.

30>25 The result will be True

9> 28 The result will be False

4.　　Operator <: This type of operator is the one that will evaluate if the value entered on the left side has a lower position than the value positioned on the right side. E.g.

26<9 Result will be False

14 < 22 The result will be True

5.　　Operator >=: This type of operator is in charge of evaluating whether the value entered on the left side has a position greater than or equal to that of the value positioned on the right side. E.g.

20> 14 The result will be True

10 > 26 The result will be False

10 >= 10 The Result will be True

6. Operator <=: This type of operator is the one that will evaluate if the value entered on the left side has a position less than or equal to the value positioned on the right side. E.g.

20 < 11 The result will be False

16 < 25 The result will be True

15 <= 15 The result will be True

- Assignment operators: These types of operators are those that are used in the program to assign (as its name says) a value to a variable, in this case, these operators will be followed by a symbol of equality (=)

1. Operator Equality (=): This type of operator is considered the main one and will always be positioned on the left side of the variable. E.g.

> A= 10 → The value of A will be 10

2. Operator Sum - equality (+=) This type of operator is responsible for adding to the variable on the left side, with the value located on the right side. E.g.

> A= 10; A += 8 → A= 18

It would be equivalent to expressing: A=10; A + 8 → A=18

3. Operator subtracts - equality (-=) This type of operator is the one that subtracts from the variable on the left side, with the value located on the right side. E.g.

> A= 10; A -= 8→ A= 2

It would be equivalent to expressing: A=10; A - 8 → A= 2

4. Operator Rest - equality (%=) This type of operator is responsible for returning the rest of the division on the left side, to the value located on the right side.

>A= 10; A %= 8 → A = 2

It would be equivalent to expressing A= 10; A % 8 → A= 2

5. Integer Operator - equality (//) This type of operator is responsible for calculating the integer division of the variable on the left side, with the value located on the right side.

> A= 10; A //= 8 → A= 1

It would be equivalent to expressing A= 10; A // 8 → A= 1

6. Operator Product - equality (*=) This type of operator is responsible for multiplying the variable on the left side, with the value located on the right side. E.g.

> A= 10; A *= 8 → A = 80

It would be equivalent to expressing: A=10; A * 8 → A= 80

7. Operator Division - equality (/=) This type of operator is in charge of dividing the variable on the left side, with the value located on the right side. E.g.

>A= 10; A /= 8 → A= 1,25

It would be equivalent to expressing A= 10; A * 8 → A= 1,25

8. Exponent Operator - equality (**=) This type of operator is responsible for calculating the exponent of the variable on the left side, with the value located on the right side. E.g.

>A= 10; A **= 8 → A = 100000000

It would be equivalent to expressing A= 10; A ** 8 → A= 100000000

- Special Operators: These types of operators are commonly used in program loops, to check for repeated variables and even to know if an element is stored within others.

1. Operator In: This operator will return a 'True' if an element is stored inside another. E.g.

A= [80, 40] 80 in A

The result that is going to return will be of the true type because the value 80 is positioned in A

2. Operator Is: This type of operator will return a True if its values stored in the variables are the same. E.g.

X= 80; Y= 80. → X is Y

The result to be returned will be of the True type because both variables contain the same stored value.

3. Operator Not in: This type of operator will return a True if an element is not stored inside another element. E.g.

A= [80, 40] 40 not in A.
The result that is going to return will be of the False type because the value 40 if it is positioned in A.

4. Operator Not is: This type of operator will return a True if the values stored in the variables are not equal. E.g.

X= 80; Y=40. → X not is Y

The result that is going to return will be of the True type because both variables contain stored different values, therefore, they are different.

- Arithmetic Operators: These types of operators are those used to perform simple mathematical operations.

1. Sum Operator (+): This type of operator will add values of the numerical type. E.g.

40 + 40 = 80

2. Operator subtracts (-): This type of operator will subtract values from the numerical type. E.g.

40 − 40 = 0

3. Operator multiplication (*): This type of operator will multiply numerical values. E.g.

40 * 40 = 1600

4. Operator division (/): This type of operator will be responsible for dividing numerical type values. E.g.

10 / 2 = 5

5. Exponent operator (**): This type of operator will calculate the exponent of a stored value between values with numerical data type. E.g.

4** 2 = 16

6. Integer Division Operator (//): This type of operator is responsible for calculating the integer division of a stored value with numeric data type in which only the integer part will return. E.g.

5 // 2 = 2

Note: It is important to note that, when working with two operands of the integer type, the program will assume that you want the variable to yield a result of the integer type. E.g.

If we operate A= 7 // 2 = Our result will be 3.

If you want to get the decimals as in the first example, just add at least one decimal value to either of the two operands. E.g.

G = 7.0 / 2 = 3.5

7. Operator Module: This type of operator is responsible for returning the rest of the division between the two operands. Ex,=.

7 % 2 = 1. The division module is 1

The order of precedence or priority of arithmetic operators is as follows:
1. Exponent (**)
2. Multiplication (*), Division (/), Whole Division (//), Module (%)

In line 2 we can see that the rest of the operators are grouped together, this means that they all have the same order of priority, but at the time of operating they will be resolved by that order of precedence.
Example:
When operating: 8*10/2

This means that the operation is to be carried out as follows: 8*10= 80 / 2 = 40. The result of our operation is 40.

On the other hand, this order of precedence can be manipulated by using parentheses ().

Example:

When operating 80*(10/2)

This means that the operation is to be carried out as follows: 10/2= 5 * 4 = 20.
Let's make two small examples to work with operators, let's calculate the area of a rectangle and the other is to see if the key is correct.

First example, area of the rectangle:

```
operators.py  ×

1    b=int(input("Please enter the base: "))
2    h=int(input("Please enter the height: "))
3    print("The area is "+str(b*h))
4
```

In this example, the first thing we do is to declare the variables, the first is variable b, which is related to the base, which goes through several stages, but we put it in a single line to save space.

To explain it better, the first thing we can observe is that there is an input in the declaration of both b and h, which is an input type, so that it is going to be saved as a string, for this reason, we can also observe the int function, which will turn that string into an integer, to be able to do operations on them. Do you know why is that?

Because it is impossible to add two strings, since it is very different to add 1 + 1 than "1" + "1", because the first is a sum of integers, and its result will be equal to 2, but the second we do not know, because it is a sum of ASCII characters. And well, as you can see, the same thing is done with the variable h, therefore, b and h are two integers entered by the user.

The next action is to print in screen the following string "The area is" concatenated with the string related to the multiplication of the base and the height, because it is not possible to concatenate a string with an integer, for this reason, the function str() is used.

As you can see, this is a very basic example, and here comes a question, what happens if you enter a negative value? If, for example, you enter -5 and 2, the value returned will be -10, and this is a big mistake since there are no negative areas, therefore, it is an error that our program has. The errors can be solved by using conditionals, or also with the handling of exceptions since they will take into account these cases.

Second example, key verification:

```
operators.py

1    password="12345"
2    passuser=input("Please enter the password here: ")
3    print("User "+str(password==passuser))
4
```

The first thing is that we define the password variable as a string "12345", then, the passuser variable is declared, which is related to the input function, it will show on the screen "Please enter the password here: ", the same will make in passuser is a string.

Finally, it will be printed in screen if the key is correct or not, for it, will be printed in screen "User" and this one will concatenate with the result of comparing if password is strictly equal to passuser, but in order for this to be concatenated, it will be necessary to convert this comparison into a string, because it is necessary to delimit that when some comparison is made, the return is a boolean, and it cannot be concatenated with a string, unless it is converted, due to that, we made use of the function str().

Conditionals

With the help of logical operators, and well, of logic in general, we will base ourselves in order to be able to use the instructions, because they will allow us to make more complex programs, since they allow us to set conditions, like what? Well, for example:

If it rains today, I take my sweater; if it doesn't rain, I don't take it.

In the same way, conditionals work, since an action is going to be carried out if a certain circumstance is fulfilled, but if the expected does not happen, something else will happen.

Among the conditionals, we will find the if, the else, and the elif; there are also the cases in which we use exceptions, which are used to prevent the program from collapsing.

- if statement: This is a simple conditional, if a certain circumstance happens, an action will be taken, otherwise nothing will happen and the usual or expected flow will continue. This can be used for simple programs such as access by age, How? Well, in case the client is not old enough, it will not let him get in.

The flowchart of the if conditional is as follows:

Now, the syntax of If in Python is as follows:

- If + condition: Then inside this block, with the required indentation, the following commands will be executed, obviously, if the condition is met.

Now some important things that have to be remembered when making the if blocks, in terms of syntax:

51

- The first line is always the if + condition, followed by a colon (:), since this way it is clear that a block is being started.

- The following lines indicate the instructions that will be fulfilled, but of course, obviously, they will occur in case the condition is true.

- Finally, it is the indentation that the block of instructions must have since in case these same are not placed correctly, the program will not understand what you specifically want and it will happen that it is not going to do what you requested or simply close the program.

A clearer example of the syntax is this, which will show whether a student passed an exam or not:

```
if.py        ×

1    note=input("Put your note here: ")
2    if(int(note)<5):
3        print("You didn't pass, try again")
4
```

As we can see here, a note variable was created, which is related to the input function, awaiting the note that the user obtained, this variable is of the string type.
Subsequently, we enter the conditional part, specifically the if, and the condition to compare is that, if the note that the user obtained is lower than five, then a screen will print that the user did not pass, and needs to try again. As you can see, at the part of the if condition, the int() function was used, which is needed because the note variable is a string, and a comparison of a number with a string cannot be made, therefore it is necessary to change the type of string variable to integer, in order to make the corresponding comparison.

But what if the condition is false? Can you do another action? Well, you do, since there is another statement, and it is the else, which is used when the condition of the if is false and you need to do another action, then go to the usual flow, if you want to see this statement better explained, read the following paragraphs, which are responsible for explaining the statement.

- else + condition: The else condition is used when the if condition is false, what does this mean? This is nothing more than if the clause of the condition is not fulfilled, the program will close automatically; so that this does not happen we make use of the else instruction which will tell the program to perform another action.

The flowchart of the else conditional is the following:

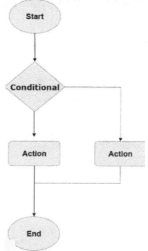

We can observe that the syntax of the conditional else is very similar to the syntax of the conditional if, only that, in this case, the conditional does not have to be placed, but it is of fundamental importance to maintain a correct indentation.

To observe in detail the programming of the else conditional, we will make a test program, in this way we will be able to see clearly the difference between conditionals.

It will be a modification to the past program, with the objective of showing how powerful the use of conditionals can be.

```
if.py
1    note=input("Put your note here: ")
2    if(int(note)<5):
3        print("You didn't pass")
4    else:
5        print("Congatulations, you pass")
6
```

In this example, we can see that the note variable was created, which is an entry that the user will choose, well, in this case, he will put his note, so that then the program will say if his note was enough to pass or not, so, to make clear to the user that he has to enter his note, the following string "Put your note here" will be printed on the screen, so the user knows that he has to put his note in the program.

After this, the conditional block was placed, in which the condition means that if the transformation to integer of the note entered by the user is less than five, "You didn't pass" will be printed on the screen, and then the program will end, since the block of the else will not be entered, because the condition is true. But if the condition is not true, it will be passed to else, which will print on the screen the next string "Congratulations, you passed", in order to show users that with their note they passed or not the exam.

As you could have observed, the use of if and else, is very useful, we would say that fundamental, because, thanks to it, you can make the program able to have different results and not have a single simple flow, because as you can guess, that type of programs that do not have logical bifurcations, are not widely used.

Another example that we can see is the division, with the same, we can see another very important utility of conditionals because the denominator cannot be equal to zero, because the division between zero is not defined and would be a mathematical error.

```python
num=input("Select the number of the numerator: ")
den=input("Select the number of the denominator: ")
if(den=="0"):
    print("Zero can't be denominator")
else:
    num=int(num)
    den=int(den)
    result=num/den
    print("The result is "+str(result))
```

Here we can see the example of the division since we have the problem previously explained.

The first thing is to create the variable num, it will be related to the numerator of the division, it will be declared next to an input function, so that the user enters the value he wants. Then the same will be done with the den variable, which is related to the denominator of the division.

Then we will enter the block of conditionals, the condition we will look for is that the variable den is equal to string "0", to know if, at the time of making the division, it can be or not. If the condition is true, the following string "Zero can't be denominator" will be printed on the screen, in order to show the user that the number he put as denominator does not meet the mathematical requirements. But, in the case that the condition is different from zero, the division can be done, therefore, we enter inside the else block; the first thing we do is to convert into integers the variable num and the variable den, but what is the objective of doing this in this part of the code? Well, to be able to do mathematical operations, both with num and den will have to be integers, but it is done in the part of the else, as a part of code optimization, because in the case that the denominator had been zero, time would have been spent on unnecessary instructions, because no operation was going to be performed, since the division between zero is not allowed, as you already know. At this moment, you will say that there is no difference between doing it here or not, but there is, imagine that you have to do that a million times, that would generate a big computational expense in something that is not going to be used, that is why it is always important to make this type of reasoning, in such a way that it is trying to make the program as optimal as possible.

The next action is to make the division between the numerator and the denominator, and this value will be stored in the result variable, to finally print the obtained result on screen.

If you are a little bit of a programmer, or already know how to program in C or Arduino, to say some languages, you will be waiting, in these explanations of the conditional sentences, the explanation of how the switch is used here, because in Python these are not found, in Python it is used the elif is used and its explanation can be seen below.

- elif + condition: We use the elif conditional as a faster and more effective way to join an else with elif for when there is more than one condition. For example: in other programming languages, it is very common to use the switch() conditional for multiple conditions. In the case of Python, this is replaced by elif(), this is nothing more than placing an additional conditional on the else to obtain multiple cases.

This is commonly used when you have multiple conditions, which have many different ways to perform.

Now, we will see an example to be able to understand in a very clear way how this works, and in this way, we will enter the conditionals.

```python
option=input("Please enter your option,for your message: \n1)Español \n2)English \n3)Deutsh \n")
if(option=="1"):
    print("Hola")
elif(option=="2"):
    print("Hello")
elif(option=="3"):
    print("Halo")
else:
    print("Bad option")
```

In the elif example, we can see that the option variable has been created, which is related to the option that the user wants to enter into his program, as can be seen in the code, the options are 1 for the answer to be in Spanish, 2 for the answer to be in English, and finally 3 for the answer of the program to be in German.

When entering the conditional block, the first thing we see is the if, which will have the condition that the variable option is the same strict as the string "1", if it is true, the string "Hello" will be shown on the screen; then, if this option is not fulfilled, it will go to the first elif, which will have a different condition, in this case is the one that says that the variable option is the same strict as the string "2", if this option is true, then it will show the message on screen, which says "Hello"; the last elif has the condition which indicates that the variable option has to be the same strict as the string "3", if it is true, it will proceed to send a message in German that says the following: "Halo". But if no case is fulfilled it will go to the else block, and this indicates that it will print in the console, a message that says "Bad option".

Therefore, we could see that the program has three options, and each one is a message that will be shown to the user saying hello in different languages, such as Spanish, German and English.

As we could see the examples of conditionals, we could see the great usefulness that they have in the programming, since they allow us to place an accumulation of options to our programs, and that they respond in a different way, depending on the situation.

But these conditionals are not the only ones that we can use for special conditions, another very useful tool, which is used a lot in programming, are the exceptions, as these catch any error, for the program to run in a correct way, moreover, in the example of division by zero you can use this tool, but not only for division by zero, but many more times, the only thing you need is the tools that you will see below.

Exception handling:

When we program, it is very frequent that we find errors during the execution of our programs. Two very common types of errors we might encounter on our way are syntax errors and exceptions. As we have already seen, syntax errors are those that occur when we enter code incorrectly.

In the case of exceptions, the syntax errors presented are different. How is this? Well, they happen while during the execution of a program something unexpected happens. For example, let's suppose a program in which we ask a user to enter a number to fill in a requirement. Now imagine that when the user is going to enter the data, he writes a string instead of a number, the program will automatically show a TypeError error.

When we don't handle exceptions properly, our program will close immediately because the interpreter won't know what to do in a special case like that.

Returning to the example shown above, we know that as long as we enter an integer value as an input value, our program will work correctly. However, if we enter a string the other type of error will be an exception to the ValueError type.

Some of the most common exceptions are:

NameError: The type of exception NameError, is the one that occurs when a program is not able to locate a global or local name. When the program is going to show us that it has not been possible to locate, it will include the wrong name in the message.

TypeError: The type of exception TypeError, is the one that occurs when an inappropriate object passes through the function as its argument. When the program is going to show us the type of error that has been presented, it will include in detail the correct ways to work with the arguments.

ValueError: The type of exception ValueError, is the one that occurs when an argument of the function contains its correct defined types, but its value is not adequate.

NotImplementedError: The type of exception NotImplementedError, is the one that occurs when an object that supports an operation has not been implemented. These types of errors are considered not to be used when a function supports an input argument, the most appropriate would be to use an exception of the TypeError type.

ZeroDivisionError: The ZeroDivisionError type of exception is one that occurs when a zero type of data is provided to the argument (such as a denominator) in a division operation or module operation.

FileNotFoundError: The FileNotFoundError exception type, is the one that occurs when a dictionary or file that has been requested is not existing in the program.

Handling exceptions: It is known that in each programming language there are certain quantities of reversed words, which make it easier for us to handle any exception that may arise when programming. In this way, we can take quick action to prevent the program from being interrupted.

In Python, when we handle exceptions we perform operations called "blocks", these blocks will be mostly used with the try, except & finally sentences.

So how does this work?
Raising the exception is going to happen in the following way: in the try block, you will find all the code, which could be raised with an exception. (It is known the term raise for programmers as the action of generating an exception.)
Once this is done, the exception block will be located, this is the one that will be in charge of enclosing the exception to obtain an opportunity to process it by sending a specific sample message.

Lastly, we have the finally block, which we are going to use to perform an action. This will be done no matter if the exception has been made or not, this way the block will be executed regardless of the previous conditions.

When we program exceptions the sentence finally is always considered very useful but many times there is not much emphasis on its importance.

Which is the finally block? What is it used for? What is it based on?

Let's suppose that we have written a code in the try block, it will take care of a certain task and will use a large amount of resources which have to be released once they cease to be used. These resources will be eliminated or released through the finally clause and the code will be executed without taking into consideration if the try block has been able to raise the exception it had.

As we know, it is not possible to make a division by zero, so we will use a similar example to show you how useful it is to work with exceptions.

```
execp.py   ×

1   num=input("Please enter the numerator: ")
2   den=input("Please enter the denominator: ")
3   den= int(den)
4   nun=int(num)
5   try:
6       result=num/den
7       print("The result is: "+ srt(result))
8   except:
9       print("Invalid values")
10
```

The first thing is to declare the variable num, which is related to the input function, it will be waiting for the data to be entered by the user, in such a way that a decimal value will be expected to be stored in num; in an analogous way, the same is done with the variable den, which is designed to be the denominator of the division.

The following action to all this, is to change the type of format of each variable, for it is used the function int(), to convert the variable num and den to integers, since as they are related to an input, the same ones will be stored as a string and it will be impossible to make arithmetic operations with them, for this reason, they are transformed to variables of type int.
Now we will enter the exceptions, since we first enter the try block, which is in charge, as its name indicates, of trying to do certain actions, if no exception occurs; what we mean by this is that, in this case, if den is not equal to zero, no exception should occur, therefore, the value of the division between num and den should be stored in the variable result, then the value of it will be printed on screen.

But in the case that some error occurs, specifically some exception, it will enter in the exceptions and will proceed to print in screen that the entered values are not valid.

Another example that we must show, is one which takes the block finally, so we can see its functionality, for this, we will continue with the examples of divisions, but now we are going to put two exceptions, one that will appear in the case that the values that are entered are not decimal, therefore, it will be impossible to convert these data into integers, for this reason, the first exception will be triggered. Then it will be verified if the denominator is equal to zero, and if it is true, another exception will have to be thrown.

```python
num=input("Please enter the numerator: ")
den=input("Please enter the denominator: ")
try:
    den= int(den)
    num=int(num)
except:
    print("Error, you put a ASCII data, please try again")
    num=int(input("Please enter the numerator: "))
    den=int(input("Please enter the denominator: "))
try:
    result=num/den
    print("The result is: "+str(result))
except:
    print("Error, the den has a value equal to zero")
finally:
    print("Thanks for use this program")
```

Here we can see better the example, the first thing we see, and that we should expect, is that both the variable num, and the variable den, are using the input() function, which will be in charge of receiving the value that the user wants, in this case, the value of the numerator and the denominator respectively.

Then we enter the first block of instructions, What are we trying to do in this section? The first thing is to convert the strings that are both num and den, to integer variables in order to continue with the relevant mathematical operations, for this reason, it is important to make the type transformation, because as you know, it is not possible to

62

divide a letter between another letter, because mathematically it does not make sense. The first thing is the try block, which as its name indicates, will try to do something, if there is not anything that generates some error, then it will do it without any problem, but in the case that it is not possible to do that, then it will enter inside the block except, which will be in charge of processing the exception. That block, in case, that an error has been found, will enter in action since it will try to fix the error found, the first thing it will do is to show in screen the error, it will transmit to you that erroneous ASCII data was placed, that please try again. Then the num variable will be Redeclared, which will be input type since it will be waiting for the values entered by the user, and then it will be transformed to an integer type variable, the same will be done with the den variable.

Later, the other block of exceptions will be entered, the first instruction we find in it is to declare the result variable, which will be the division between the num and den; to then place on the screen the result of the division. And well, as you should know, this block will try to do that, but there is the possibility of an error, but what could it be? Well, the main one is the division by zero, more than a programming error, it is a mathematical error, therefore, this block cannot be executed and the part of the exception will be entered. The same one will try to communicate to the user that an error exists, this message will say to him that the denominator has a value equal to zero, for this reason, it is not going to be possible to execute the division.

At last, we will enter the finally block, which will make an instruction no matter what happens, no matter if the try or the excepts are executed, this block will always be executed. It, in this case, will print a message, in which it will be thankful to have used this program.

But if you verify the previous example and this one, the block finally does not do anything very special, but it does, the difference is that this is always done, now, if you want to get an example, in which is used more and is more important the finally, you will see it when you use the databases, because always, whatever happens, it is essential to close the connection to a database, because if this is not done, it may cause some errors that any programmers want to have.

Chapter 4: Loops

What is a Loop?

A loop (or cycle), is a control structure that is in charge of repeating a block of instructions, while a certain condition is fulfilled, within the loops we also have the so-called infinite loops in which their condition is never fulfilled. As in most programming languages, Python has a while and for.

> 1.   Loop For: Python's for statement iterates on the items of any sequence (either a list, a string of characters or dictionary), in the order they appear in the sequence. Where the code is called "loop body" and its repetitions "iterations".

Where iteration is defined by performing a number of actions repeated times. The for loop is in charge of going through these actions in order to look for elements that fulfill certain conditions and that at the same time can carry out the specified instructions. So all these elements must be iterable.
The syntax of a for loop is as follows:
for variable + an iterable element (list, string, range, etc.) : loop body.
It is necessary to specify the variable in which the items of the element are going to be saved, then we write our sentence for with a variable that will store the items and finally we write in which will be our element to iterate.

The loop is executed as long as it fulfills a condition, so once the iteration is finished, this will make the loop stop.

Example:

```
1    x=0
2    for x in range(4):
3        print(x)
4    print("End")
5
```

The first thing we can see is that we define the variable x, which starts at zero, this is because it is going to iterate, and must start with zero.

Then we fully enter the for cycle, and as you can see, it is specified that the variable x, is going to iterate within the range of 4, What does this mean? Well, x is going to iterate four times and take the value of zero, one, two and three.
The next part is the block inside the for, which is a simple print, and this is going to show us the value that has x in each part of the for, until it gets to be valued four, when it has that value, it will automatically quit the cycle.

Finally, End will be written to show that the program is finished and the cycle was quit.

Types of for loops:

1. Loop "for" with lists: you can make for cycles with lists, in this case, it will iterate within each value of the list.
In order to better understand what we are talking about, we will make some examples of each one of these ways of using the for.

> a.   Loop "for" with list and the function "range"; in this loop are presented list data types and with the help of the function len() and range(), it is possible to make a for, these are very useful to print data.

-range() is a function that, as mentioned above, returns a list of integers, accepting as arguments the beginning of the list,

the end and the increment between one element and the next. We can also omit one or two of them, as explained below;
- range (n); this type of function takes care of returning a list of integers beginning with 0 and ending in n-1.
- range (beginning, end); this type of function is in charge of returning the list of integers located between the beginning and the end, without including the latter.
- range (beginning, end, step); this type of function takes charge of returning the list of integers, as in the previous case, only that between the beginning and the next element will exist a difference of step, and so on.

Let's do two examples, one without the range function, and another with it.

1)   Use of for and lists, without the use of range:

```
sports=['soccer', 'baseball','tennis','polo']
for x in sports:
    print(x)
print("End")
```

As you can see in the example, first, a list was created, which has the name sports, it has as items, different sports, such as soccer, baseball, tennis, and polo.

Subsequently, the for cycle was defined, and, What does the x variable do this time? What it does is iterate within the sports list, so x will take the values of each item it has within the list.

The next thing is to define the for block, it is important to remember the indentation because if this is not done, no action will be done because Python takes this very seriously. Since we already placed the indentation, we define the block, which is a simple print, and what this does is print the values of x, and well, as we have already explained, x will take the value of the items from the list in question.

And well, to finish, will be printed on-screen "End", to show that the program has finished and quit the cycle correctly.

2)   Use of for and lists, with the use of range:

```
for.py

1    sports=['soccer', 'baseball','tennis','polo']
2    for x in range(len(sports)):
3        print("The sport "+str(x+1)+" is "+sports[x])
4    print("End")
5
```

In the example, we can see a change; the first one is that in this case we use the range, but we are going to go step by step to explain the code and make it very simple.
The first thing, as we have already seen, is to make a list, in this case, the same list of the previous example, with the consequences that this entails, this means that the items of the previous example, will be the same as the current ones.

Then, we define the for, in this case, we place the range, with which we mean that x iterate from zero to the range of numbers that the len function returns to us, but, what does this mean? Well, x is going to iterate within a list of the length that the len function tells us, therefore, if len returns a value of four, then the variable x will iterate from zero to three, taking the values zero, one, two, three, and as you can see, it will iterate four times, as the len function said, of course, if it gives us a value of four.

Afterward, we programmed the for block, which is a print, but in this case, "The sport" was printed, then it was concatenated with the string that returned the function str(x+1), but, why x+1? Because as x varies from zero to the number that gives us the function range, the first position of the sport will be zero, for that reason, we added one, and so it will appear on the

68

screen, that the first sport, is in position one. After this, it is concatenated with " is " and it is also concatenated with sport[x], in this case, as if it is a list, it is concatenated with the item of the position x of the list, and these positions go from zero to the value n-1 of range.

And finally, "End" was printed on the screen, to say that the program has finished, and the for cycle was finished correctly.

It is important to remember, that for the variable x to vary, this has to iterate within a list, and as it has been said before, the function range returns a list of m numbers, therefore if we say that a = range(10), we can obtain that a will be equal to [0, 1, 2, 3, 4, 5, 6, 7, 8, 9], therefore, the variable x will vary from zero to nine.

b.   Loop "for" with Tuples; tuples are sequence objects, specifically, it is an immutable list data type, so it cannot be modified after its creation. This type of program is not very difficult to design, since, to program in tuples and cycles, it is done in a similar way that with lists, the only detail is to keep in mind the difference that exists between list and tuple.

Two examples will be shown in the same way, the first one will be with range and the other one will obviate this function.

1)   Loop for with Tuples and range:

```
for.py          ×

1    foods=("pizza", "hot dog", "sushi")
2    x=0
3    for food in range(len(foods)):
4        print("The x value is: "+str(x))
5        print("The food value is: "+str(food))
6        print("The foods item is: "+foods[food])
7        x+=1
8    print("End")
9
```

Here the first thing we see is that we create the tuple foods, which has some items within it, among which are the strings "pizza", "hot dog" and "sushi", and as you should know, after creating a tuple, it cannot be modified, or changed, or anything like that.

Then a variable x was declared, which has the assigned value of zero.

Next step is to declare the for, and as you can see, in this case, it is not going to iterate the variable x, but a food variable, which is going to iterate within the list that is going to return the range function, which should give a list of three elements, and, Why three elements? Well, as you already know, the len function returns the value of the length of a list or a tuple, and as in this case, the tuple foods has three elements, then the range function should create a tuple that goes from zero to two.

Then, to see more clearly how the variable food iterates, the following instructions were programmed, first the value that has the variable x was printed in that instant, then, the value of food was printed in that instant, with the objective of verifying if they have the same value, and as you already know, to concatenate an integer with a string, the function str was used. Next act is to print the item of the corresponding food, for that reason "The food item is: " is concatenated with foods[food], since we can select a specific value of the tuple foods, and well, in this case, it will be the one that is in the food position. Last but not least, it is said that x will be updated to the next value.

To finalize the code, the string "End" will be printed in the console, to make it clear that the program has finished and that it ended in a correct way.

2) Loop for with Tuples and without range:

```
for.py            ×

1    messages=("Hello", "my", "name", "is", "Marco")
2    for message in messages:
3        print(message)
4    print("End")
5
```

In this example, we can see that it is very nice since we send a message with the tuple, but how does this work? Well...

First, we create the tuple messages, which has the following items, "Hello", "my", "name", "is", "Marco", as we can see, is a tuple of five items, therefore it has a length of five.

Next step is to create the for, in this case, the variable message, it will iterate inside the tuple messages; Then the variable message will be printed, in the position that it is, with which, you will be able to infer that each message will be printed with a line break.

And finally, as it has been done in the previous examples, it will be printed in console "End' to show that it has left the cycle and the program is finished.

>c. Loop "for" with dictionary; the dictionary defines a one-to-one relationship between keys and values, the dictionary type objects allow a series of operators integrated in the Python interpreter for its management.

Analogous to the loops explained above, this "for" loop with dictionary is worked in a very similar way, since all these types of data are similar. But it is worth mentioning that they are different types and are treated in a different way, therefore, even if they are handled similarly, it should never be forgotten that they are different types of data.

Example:

```
for.py          ●

1    clothes={"shirt":"red", "shoes":"black","pant":"blue"}
2    for key in clothes:
3        print(key)
4    clothe=input("Choose one of them: ")
5    if(clothe in clothes):
6        print("Your clothe is "+clothe+ " of color "+clothes[clothe])
7    else:
8        print("Error")
9
```

In this example we can see how to work with dictionaries; with the variable we created called clothes, which, as you know, is a dictionary. This has the items "shirt", which has a value associated with "red", there is also "shoes", which is related to "black", and finally "pant", which relates to "blue".

After that, we created the for cycle, which tells us that the key variable will iterate in all the values of the clothes dictionary. And if you run this code, in your favorite text editor, you will note that the key variable, will only have associated the values of "shirt", "shoes" and "pant", this can be observed, because the cycle inside the for, what it does is to print the key-value inside the dictionary.

Then, we create the clothe variable, which is a variable that will receive an input, which will depend on the user. When receiving the user's value, an if will be made, and in the case that the variable clothe is inside clothes, as you can see in the condition of the if, it will be entered there, and it will be printed that "Your clothe is" + the option chosen by the user + "of color "+ clothes[clothe]; but what are clothes[clothe]? It is the value associated with the clothe selected by the user, better said, if the user chooses "pant", then clothes[clothe] will throw the value of "blue".

Finally, the else condition means that if no clothe is found inside clothes, then "Error" will be printed, and this is very useful since if no value is found inside a database, it will be thrown that the requested value is found or not.

> 2.   Loop "While"; it allows us to execute cycles or periodic sequences that allow us to do things multiple times in a row. This cycle will allow us to execute a block continuously, as long as the while condition is true, and by this, we mean "True". This loop will be in charge of evaluating the condition and if it is correct, the loop is executed and the condition is checked again at the end and if it is still true "True", the program will be executed again, if this condition is not correct "False", it will be omitted and the common execution of the program will be carried out.

There are several types of "while" loops; like the "while" loop controlled by counting, the infinite while and others; all very useful in specific conditions.

Its syntax is very simple, and is as follows:
While (condition):
Block of instructions within the cycle

Now let's make a simple example, which will consist of the cycle printing a number, as many times as the user wants.

Example:

```
Welcome        while.py    ×

1    cycles=input("Put the number of cycles here: ")
2    count=0
3    while(count<int(cycles)):
4        count+=1
5        print("Cycle number "+str(count))
6    print("End")
7
```

In this example, we can observe several things, the first is that we create a variable cycles, which is an entry, which will allow us, as users to enter the number of cycles we want to do in this program, of course, you must never forget that this type of entry is a string, therefore, to do mathematical operations, it is necessary to transform this type of input.

Then another variable will be created, called count, which has a fundamental function, and it is to be the cycle counter of our program, with which we define that the same one will begin in zero, for then, to start the count.

The next action is, to begin with the while cycle, as we can see in the syntax previously explained, first it is declared that we are going to make a while, then, between the parentheses we have the condition.

    a.   Loop "while" controlled by counting; in this cycle, there is a counter, and this counter will increase as the cycles are carried out, this process will be repeated as many times as necessary until the expected number is reached. We will understand this loop better with the example that we will see next.

Although we have already seen an example of the while controlled by counting, that was the last one, it is never too much to take another example, the same through the counting method, in this case, we are going to make the counter go from higher to lower, as we will see below.

```
while.py     ✕

1    cycles=input("Put the number of cycles here: ")
2    a=int(cycles)
3    while(0<a):
4        a-=1
5        print("Cycles to end "+str(a))
6    print("End")
7
```

In this example, we make a turn of one hundred and eighty degrees, because the counter does not have to reach the maximum value, but starts in it and is going to decrease.

The first thing is that a variable called cycles is created, which is related to an input that the user will write, in which he will enter the number of cycles he wants to do. Next act is to create a variable a, which needs the function int(), since it turns the variable cycles into an integer, because as you should know, the variable cycles is a string, since the entries are saved that way, and with the strings it is not possible to perform arithmetic operations.
In the following line, we declare the while loop, and as it can be observed, the condition is that zero has to be lower strictly than a, therefore, in the moment that a is equal to zero, the cycle will be exited and the other instruction will be passed.

Then, inside the block of instructions that are inside the cycle, the variable a has to be decreased, this is done through the instruction a-=1, which is equivalent to saying that a = a -1, and it can be observed easily as the variable a is decreased by a unit.

The next instruction is to print on screen the following message "Cycles to end" concatenated with the number of missing cycles to exit the cycle.

Finally, the "End" string is placed on the screen to say that the program has finished and that the while was exited correctly.

This type of cycles by counts are very useful, we are going to use them first with the utility of those cycles in which it is necessary that the counter grows, the first utility that comes to our head is to make a programmed chronometer, in such a way that when arriving at the maximum value, it is going to leave the cycle and show in screen that the required time has been fulfilled, now, there are also other utilities as it can be to check a list with a known length, therefore we will be moving item by item; although this last utility easily can be replaced by a loop for. Now, while cycles per count, but in this case, that the counter goes decreasing, could be used to make a countdown to sound an alarm or something like that.

b.   Infinite "while" loop: This type of while is very useful, in the case that an accumulation of instructions is done a number of times not determined, with this we mean that we do not know how many times it is going to be done, therefore the programmer, will make the condition a while(True), and of course, as you can see, the True boolean, allows the while to work constantly. Let's code two examples, one that we use an infinite while, the strict way, and another not so much, although the programmer does not know the number of cycles that will be done, does not use the True condition to force the block to be repeated indefinitely.

Examples:
        1)   While with the True condition:

```
while.py    ×

1    import time
2    x=1
3    while(True):
4        print(x)
5        x+=1
6        time.sleep(1)
7
```

The first thing we observe that is different is the import of the time module, but those are issues that we will see later, at this time is not something very important.

Now what really interests us is the declaration of the variable x as one since this will work as a kind of counter, so it will increase little by little.

The next step is to create or, better said, declare the while, and as you can see, the condition inside the while is True, therefore, it will always be fulfilled, which indicates that the cycle will be repeated at all times, unless some sentences are declared, which we will see later.

Inside the while block, the variable x will be printed on the screen, and this is where it makes sense to use x as a counter since it will allow us to see in the console the specific second that has happened since the program started. Then it increases the value of x, because as we have already said, it has a counter function, and it will increase one by one.

Finally, we use the library time, so that will make a delay of a second, that's why our program works as a chronometer, which will show us on screen the second in which we are after running the code, and the same will be updated every second.

Sentences used in the while loop:

1. Break Sentence: the word break is used to interrupt the cycles or abandon the cycles even when they have not finished, meaning that the evaluated expression of while remains in the true position. To be able to evaluate and understand this sentence, let's see the following example.

2.

```
while.py    ×

1    while True:
2        x=input("Put one to break of the while cycle: ")
3        if(x=="1"):
4            break
5        print("You dont put the one, please try again")
6    print("End")
7
```

In this example, we see how to implement infinite while cycles, because as you can see in the first line, the condition inside the while is always going to be true, therefore we are in front of an infinite cycle.

Later, we declare the variable x, which is related to the input function, which will be waiting for the user to enter any value, specifically, it is necessary to enter a one so that it exits the cycle, in case that what user enters is not the indicated value, then the cycle will be repeated.

As you can see in line three, you have a statement of an if, which asks if x is equal to the string "1", Why is it compared with a string? Because, as we already know, x is a string because it is related to the input function, at the moment in which this variable is declared. If the condition is true, the "break" sentence will be used, which specifies us to exit the infinite cycle.

If the condition is not true, then the following string "You don't put the one, please try again" will be printed on the screen.

Finally, at the moment of exiting the cycle, the usual "End" will be printed, to show that the cycle was executed correctly, and the program was finished.

What we can learn from our example with the break? or what benefit we can get from it? Well, the first thing is that the sentence break is extremely useful to get out of the cycles, it does not have to be strictly an infinite cycle, because it can be used in a cycle that is operated by counting or another method, therefore, it is important to remember that. Another fundamental thing is that this type of sentence, not only works for a while but can also be used in for cycles, therefore, are an essential tool when programming.

But in what cases should this type of statement be used? Well, the first case that comes to mind is the handling of some exception that may occur within the cycles, in the event that something unwanted occurs, it gets out of it and notifies the error or does what you desire to program. Another case may be an access system since a specific key was requested, and in the case that the correct key is not entered, the user will not be allowed to enter another part of the program.

> 3.   Sentence Continue: This sentence ends up being very useful when programming, when applying it we will be omitting what follows the sentence within the cycle. That is to say, if we fulfill some previous conditions, as, for example, if after several "if" or else, or other steps, we manage to reach a continue sentence, we will proceed to omit the rest of the instructions of the cycle, and then do another iteration. We could summarize that the instruction continues inside a loop forces the interpreter to return to the beginning of the loop ignoring all the instructions and interactions that are inside it.

79

The next example will show a while cycle, which will omit the values that are multiples of five, if these values are multiples, then it will not be printed on screen and the next iteration will be done automatically.

```
while.py
1   cycles=input("Please put the numer of cycles: ")
2   count=1
3   while(count-1<int(cycles)):
4       a=count
5       count+=1
6       if(a%5 == 0):
7           print("Error, continue")
8           continue
9       else:
10          print("Not is multiple of 5")
11      print(a)
12   print("End")
13
```

To start, the variable cycles is created, which is an input, which asks the user to enter the number of cycles he wants to do, and, as is well known, you have that cycles is a string.
Next, it creates the variable count, which is integer type, this will have the function of counter, to know the cycle in which we are, to reach the maximum level that the user wants.

Now we will create the while loop, which specifies that count-1 has to be lower than cycles, and, Why count -1? Well, in order to fulfill what the user wants; since if the condition was, a lower or equal to cycles, the code will be less optimal, for this reason, only a strict lower is placed, and as the counter starts in one, it is necessary to subtract a unit and that the number of corresponding cycles is met.

In the following line, the variable a is declared, which has the same count value, because to know the current value of the cycle, and well, as it is obvious, the counter is increased by one

unit, through the instruction in line five, which says count +=
1.

Subsequently, one enters the block of conditionals, in this
case, the condition is a% 5 ==0, but what does this mean?
Well, the rest that gives the division between a and five, has to
be strictly equal to zero, in order to enter the if. In the case
that the condition is true, the orders found in the if block will
be performed, these instructions are the following; the first
thing is to print on screen that there was an error, then the
continue sentence will be used. If this condition is false, the
instruction containing the else block will be passed, which is
based on notifying that the cycle is a multiple of five.

At the end of the conditionals, the cycle number is printed on
the screen to know when we are in the program.

And finally, a screen print is placed to show that the program
has been completed and the cycle was exited correctly.

Now, what can we learn from this program? The first thing is
the use of the continue, because its function, specifically is to
go directly to the next while cycle, omitting the other lines of
the block, well, in this case, it is the same, since when arriving
at the continue we pass to the other cycle, but in the case that
this sentence is not found, the value of a would be printed, as
you can see that it is the next instruction after the conditional
block, but this type of sentences, interrupt the natural flow of
the program, being very useful for the handling of some
exception that happens within the cycles.

4.   Pass Sentence: It is a null expression, in other
words, this sentence does nothing, but it allows us to
create a loop without placing code in its body to be able
to add it later and use it in this way as a temporary
filler, with this we mean to add some type of delay to
the program; or as well in the case that you manage the
programming with assembler or with processors, it is a
way to make a nop. It is a sentence that will not affect

in anything the behavior of the code, and it should be noted that not only can be used in cycles, it can also be used anywhere in the code without any problem, with these words, we mean that the sentence can also be used in a common function without any trouble, but this is not worth to mention yet, because we have not seen functions, but it is not excessive to know that the pass can be implemented with the functions. We could say to establish a difference that continues will take care of ending the current interaction, but will continue with the next iteration of that loop, going back to the beginning, while pass is not going to do anything, just continue with the following instructions without going back to the beginning. Next, let's see an example of what it is.

5.

```
while.py    ×

1    cycles=input("Please put the numer of cycles: ")
2    count=1
3    while(count-1<int(cycles)):
4        a=count
5        count+=1
6        if(a%5 == 0):
7            print("Error, continue")
8            pass
9        else:
10            print("Not is multiple of 5")
11        print(a)
12    print("End")
13
```

By looking at the previous example, we can see how we declare the variable cycles, which is going to wait for the user to specify how many cycles to use, the input will be of the string type.

Then the count counter will be created, which will start from one for convenience, but has the function of knowing what is the current position of the cycle.

The following order, is the creation of the while cycle, with the condition that count-1, has to be strictly lower than int(cycles), it is worth noting that the use of the int() function, since the cycles variable is of string type and making comparisons with strings and integers is not possible since they are different types of data. The reason of the count- 1 is explained in the previous example, so we don't have to repeat it, but remember that we are making comparisons starting from zero and that is the reason why the comparison is strictly lower and is not lower or equal since we would make one more cycle.

The following instructions are to declare the variable a, which will be assigned the value of count, this is to be able to make operations on this value and not lose it; then the value of count will be increased by one unit, since if this variable is not increased, we will be doing the same thing infinitely.

The next part is the conditional phase, which is in charge of verifying if it is a multiple of five, and we do this by using the "%" operator since it will return the rest of the division we place, so that if we place, for example 10% 3, it will return the value of 1, which is the rest; in an analogous way it is done here, since when putting the following instruction a% 5, we are asking for the rest between these values, and to know if a number is a multiple of another, because the rest between both should be zero, for this reason, the strict equality is made to zero, in the case that the condition is fulfilled, because we will be in front of a number that is divisible by five, or multiples of five, being those the numbers that we want to find.

Now in such a case that the if condition is met, we will proceed to make a cumulus of instructions, the same will be, to print in screen that an error has been produced and that it is going to continue, then, the following instruction is the sentence pass, which will not do anything, is like causing a small delay in the program, depending on the frequency of the clock of the processor of our machine, but those are subjects that do not interest us very much. But, if the condition is false, then it will enter inside the block of the else, and this only will print that this number of the cycle is not multiple of the five.

Now, at the moment that the conditional block was finished, therefore, it does not matter if the condition is true or false, the number of the cycle in which we are will be printed on screen, by the command print(a), because a is the current position.

Finally, when exiting the while cycle, the "End" string will be printed on the screen, which indicates that the while loop has been correctly exited and the program has been completed.

Now, when trying to find a utility to the pass sentence, you don't really find many at this moment that you haven't seen the functions, since now it's just a delay, but it's not a delay appreciable by the user, since the computer clock frequency is in GHz, therefore it's so fast that it's not appreciable, but when you see the functions, there will be times when a complex program is being developed, and there are parts that have not been created, but for the program to work it already had to have created the functions, but the body of the functions has not yet been developed, which is why the use of these sentences is important, so that our software does not break, for saying so.

Chapter 5: Functions

A function is basically a portion or block of reusable code that performs a given task. It is a code block with an associated name, which receives arguments as input, in addition, follows a sequence of sentences, which executes a desired operation and then returns a value and perform a task, this block can be called when we need, and this can be considered a great advantage. Python is a language that gives us a lot of flexibility when creating these functions.

The use of these functions is a very important component within the paradigm of programming called structured and therefore has several advantages:

* It allows reusing the same function in different programs, therefore, when it does the functions, it is not necessary to repeat the code a lot of times.
* It allows segmenting a complex program in modules that are simpler, and in this way, we will have an easier programming, as well as a more facilitated debugging, it is as the saying goes, "Divide and conquer", therefore, it is a very used technique.

The Python programming language has what we call functions integrated into the language, which allows us to create functions defined by the user himself to be used later in his own program. These functions are presented below:

Function	Use	Example	Result
Print ()	This function allows the program to print in screen the desired argument	Print ("Hello")	"Hello"

Len ()	This function allows you to determine the length of the characters that a string contains	Len ("Hello world")	11
Join()	This function allows you to convert a string to another by using "-"	List=['Python', 'is'] '-'. Join (List)	'Python-is'
Split()	This function will let you convert a string into a list	A=("This will be a list") List2= a.split()	A=['This', 'will', 'be', 'a', 'list']
Replace()	This function, as it names indicates, will let you replace a string for another	Text= "The house is green" Print (Text) Text= Text.replace("green", "yellow") Print(Text)	"The house is green" "The house is yellow"
Upper() and lower()	This function allows us to convert into upper or lower case all the	Text= "The house is green" Text.upper() Print (Text) Text.lower() Print(Text)	"THE HOUSE IS GREEN" "the house is green"

	letters in a string		
Ord()	This function will let you use ASCII data type	Print (ord('A'))	65
Tuple()	This function will convert a string into a tuple	Words= tuple ("I am old") Print(Words)	('I', 'a', 'm', 'o', 'l', 'd')
Type()	This function will return the type of data of an element	X=5 Print(type(X))	<class 'int'>
List ()	This function will let you create lists from an element	Word= list('Hello') Print (Word)	['H', 'e', 'l', 'l', 'o']
Round ()	This function will round the decimal part of a number to its nearest integer	Print (round(15,746))	16
Str()	This function will convert a numerical value into a string	X=5 A=str(X) Print (A)	"5"

Range()	This function will create a list of n elements. It is mainly used in the for cycle	X=range(3) Print(X)	[0, 1, 2]
Float ()	This function will allow us to convert any value to a decimal type of value	A=float("5.55") Print(A)	5.55
Max() & Min()	These functions will determinate the higher and the lower values in a set of numbers	X= [2, 6, 3, 8, 0] Print (max(X)) Print(min(X))	8 0
Sum()	This function will add the numbers of a set of numbers	X=[3, 1, 6] Print(sum(X))	10
Int()	This function will convert any value into an integer	A=("35") Print (int(A))	35

What rules do I have to follow to be able to define a function?

- The input parameters must be defined within the parenthesis of the function.
- When we develop the code, we must identify the indentation very well and correctly (4 characters of space).
- The code of the function will always start after we place the colon. ": "

It should be noted that a function will not be executed until it is invoked, and to be able to invoke a function it must be called by its name. For example:

```
function.py
1    a=[1, 2, 3, 4, 5]
2    b=[1, 0, 1, 0, 1]
3    num="5 6 7 8 9"
4    c=num.split()
5    print(c)
6    e=[]
7    for x in c:
8        d=int(x)
9        e.append(d)
10   c=e
11   d=[]
12   for x in range(len(a)):
13       e=a[x]+b[x]+c[x]
14       d.append(e)
15   e=min(d)
16   f=max(d)
17   g=sum(d)
18   print(a)
19   print(b)
20   print(c)
21   print(d)
22   print(e)
23   print(f)
24   print(g)
25
```

As we can see in this example, which is quite complete, at first we created variables a and b, they are lists, which have within them integer values, specifically five items, a is a list of numbers ranging from one to five, while b is an iteration of values of ones and zeros.

The second, is the creation of the variable num, it is a string, in which is written "5 6 7 8 9", and as we saw previously, the function split(), creates an arrangement of strings, each item will be a word, separated by white space, in the code, specifically in line four, we make use of this function, in which we convert the variable c, in a list of strings, which should have the form ["5", "6", "7", "8", "9"], but it is not possible to do mathematical operations with this type of data, as they are, to be more specific, as strings, therefore we are going to proceed to convert all these items into integers, so that you verify that it is true what we say here, we use the print of the list c, so that you can see the list of strings.

To achieve our goal, first we declare the variable e as an empty list, then we use a for cycle, in which the variable x, will iterate within the array c, which has its items as strings, therefore, within a variable d, the integer that results after applying the function int() to the element of the list c at that time. Then the value of d is added, within the list e, until the number of iterations is finished. The next action is to store in c, the list that was stored in e, in order to have a better order of the variables.

Subsequently, the variable d was assigned the value of an empty list, in order to store data within it. Then, with the help of a for, which is going to iterate as many times as the number of items in the list a, as we are going to have to move through all its items, since what we want is to create another list, which contains the sum of a, b and c, so inside the same buble, it is said that e will be equal to the sum of the item that is in position x, of lists a, b and c. After adding the three items, the append function will be used to add the value obtained to the d list.

How to create your own function?

To be able to create a function of our own, we must follow the "def" sentence and proceed to name it, except that this time it will not be the name of a predefined function, but this time it will have a name created by us.

How can I call a function?

To be able to call a function, we only have to declare it when we start in our code. This is fundamental because it is not possible to invoke a function that has not been created in advance. Example:

Parameters

We define parameters as a type of value that is entered into the function when the function is invoked, a function may be able to receive one or more parameters. These parameters must be separated by a comma "," in order to be invoked. Example:

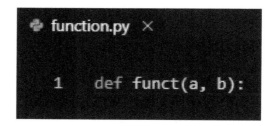

As you can see in this small example, because it is very simple, really, it was just to show how the first part of a function should be defined.

The sentence that can never be missing when defining a function is the def, which is the one that specifies that a function is going to be created or, better said, indicates that a function is being defined.

Then we can see that follows a word, in this case, funct, that word was to put a name to our function, and then you can see a parenthesis, which has two letters, a and b, meaning that these are going to be the parameters that our function will receive to work.

How can we define arguments and parameters?

As we already know, we call parameters to the values that the function receives when it is defined. When the function is invoked, these values are called arguments and divided according to their type.

These arguments are divided into several types:

Arguments by name:

When we are going to invoke a function, we must indicate in the arguments the value that each parameter will contain starting from its name.

```python
def funct(a, b):
    return a+b

c=funct(b=5, a=3)
print(c)
```

As we can see, we continue with the funct function, in this case, we still have the same parameters a and b, we also see how the definition is exactly the same, the only difference is at line two, as it indicates that the sum of a with b is going to return. The return sentence will be explained later, but it is not something too complicated, the same name tells us what it does, to return a value.

Then in the following lines, the variable c is created, which will be equal to the value returned by the function we have created, and as we said previously, it will be equal to the sum of its parameters a and b. As you can see, when you call the function in line four, first write the name of the function, in this case funct, and the arguments that are going to be passed, are previously specified with the name, as you can see, the argument that has a value of five, is specified that it will be parameter b of the funct function, analogously is done with parameter a.

Finally, the value of c is printed on the screen, so that you can visualize that the result is correct.

Argument by position:

When we send an argument to a function, they receive the defined parameters in order.

```
function.py ×

1    def hello(name, color):
2        print("Hello "+name+ " your favorite color is "+color)
3
4    a=input("What is your name? ")
5    b=input("What is your favorite color? ")
6    hello(a,b)
7
```

In this example, another function will be created, which is called hello, and has as parameters both name and color, this function was created to make a message on screen, in which the user will be greeted with his name and will also be told what is his favorite color.

To call this function first it is necessary to declare two variables, the first one is the variable a, who is in charge of storing the value of the string related to the user's name, while b, is in charge of storing the string related to the user's favorite color, these variables are related to the input function, which means that they will be waiting for the user to enter the value he wants.

Finally, the hello function is called, making use of its name, but in this case, the arguments were passed by order and not by name, so you have to be very aware for the correct order, since, if there is an error in this, the program can easily collapse or fail to do what is required.

As you could see, the ways to pass the arguments are different, you can use the one you prefer, it depends on your preferences; in the case that you find it easier or faster by position do it that way, but take into account that you have to be aware that the argument is in the correct parameter position, but if you like it more by name, do it that way, of course, you also have to be aware that you are writing the parameter names correctly.

Call without arguments

When we call a function that has some defined parameters, if these are not passed correctly an error will be generated.

In this example, the hello function is created, which is not going to have parameters, and this will only make a screen print, with the message "Hello".
Then, to call it, only the name of the function will be written with parentheses, in the following way name().

Return statement

As we have seen before, most Python functions will contain a return value which can be explicit or implicit.

We know that return is a reserved word whose purposes are to finish the execution of some function and then return the value obtained as a result.

If you want to visualize an example of this, you can see the one that is in arguments by position, since it can be observed that the function has the return sentence, which will return the value of the sum of a plus b; and also, as you can observe in this example, that value is stored in the variable c, to then print it.

Lambda function

We define lambda functions as a special type of function which is part of the predefined functions in Python. What do we mean by this? This type of function is mainly noted for being "exclusive" because it allows us to create "anonymous" functions quickly because it has a somewhat exclusive syntax.

The lambda functions are able to execute an expression and return the result of it, it can contain optional parameters in its structure, but nevertheless, this function has its own restrictions.

Syntax of the lambda function

The syntax of the lambda function in Python is very simple since it is based only on writing the reserved word lambda, followed by the arguments that come with the action and finally separating with their respective double point ":".

```
function.py ✕

1    sum= lambda x,y: x+y
2    a=sum(3,10)
3    print(a)
```

In this example, we see the use of the function lambda, in this case to the variable sum, we make use of the sentence lambda, in order to create a function that has as purpose to make the sum of two numbers, both x and y. For that reason, it is observed that the parameters that we have is the one of x and y; for then inside the block of the function, return the sum of both.

Finally, to call the function, to the variable that we declared as a, we assigned the value that returns sum, for then, to make sure that the result is certain, we proceeded to print in screen the value that stores the variable a, and if you get to run this program, you will be able to observe that it will give 13.

The lambda function is commonly used when you need to invoke a function for a short time (this function does not require a name) and is mostly used together with the integrated functions filter(), map().

Filter() function

The filter() function is the one (as its name indicates) that is in charge of filtering. What does this mean? This function takes a sequence as arguments, either a list or an iterator, then it will return an iterable with the elements already filtered (this will return a true if the condition is met).

```python
def pair(n):
    if(n>0 and n%2==0):
        return True
    else:
        return False

numbers=[]
for x in range(25):
    numbers.append(x)

pairs=filter(pair, numbers)

for x in pairs:
    print("The number "+str(x)+" is pair")
```

For this example, the first thing we need is a conditional function, to know what we are going to filter, in our case, we will create the pair function, which will have as parameter, the integer n, then we enter a conditional block, in the part of the if, the condition would be that n has to be higher than zero, since the zero is a number that is not even, the other condition that must be fulfilled at the same time, is that the rest of the division between n and two has to be strictly equal to zero, because as you should know, this is the definition of a pair number.

The next step is to fill our arrangement of numbers that we are going to filter, for it we create the variable numbers, which will be an empty list. To then enter a for loop, in which a variable x will vary from zero to 24, as you can see in line 8, this is thanks to the range function, which gives us the limits of the for. The next thing to do is to fill in our list, this is done using the append function, in the numbers variable, which, if you remember is an empty list, after it is filled in, it already becomes a list with integer values as items.

We are already able to filter the list, and we do it creating a list called pairs, which will use the filter function, and the same one will return the values of the arrangement that the function returns to us as True, as for example 2, since this one is higher than zero and the module of the division of the same one, between two is equal to zero, therefore, it fulfills the requirements.

The last step is to print in screen all the obtained pairs, and we do it with the help of another cycle for, in which a variable x, will iterate through all the list and will print us that those numbers are even.

Function map()

The map() function is the one that is in charge of executing each element on a list or tuple to be able to return a sequence of elements which will be the result of the operation.

```
function.py ×

1    def sum(a, b):
2    |    return a + b
3
4    list1=[1, 0, 1, 0, 1]
5    list2=[0, 2, 0, 2, 0]
6    c=map(sum, list1, list2)
7    print(list(c))
8
9    string1=["Hello, ", "are "]
10   string2=["how ","you"]
11   c=map(sum, string1, string2)
12   print(list(c))
```

In this example, we can see in the first lines, the definition of a function called sum, which has as parameters, variables a and b do not have to be exclusively integers, they can be strings or any other type of data. It will return a+b, whether it is a concatenation or a sum.

Later, we created two lists, the "List1" and the "List2", the same, are lists that have within them, an iteration of numbers between one and zero, this is for List1, now for the case two it is analogous, but in this case, are iterations between the numbers two and zero.

Then, we declare a variable c, it will make use of the map function, and will receive as arguments, the function sum, list1, and list2, what this will do is to create a list that will be in a specific memory address, which will have as items, the sum of list1 and list2. To print what is in c, it is important to use the list() sentence, since if you want to show the desired data, we have to tell the program that we want to see the list that is in that memory address.

Later, two variables were defined, the first is string1 and the second is string2, which will have a message. After the declarations, the map variable is used, and it receives the parameters sum, string1 and string2, what we are doing in this case, is concatenating the strings that there are as item of each list. Finally, we will print in screen the value of the list that is in the address c.

What are the differences between the lambda functions and the functions defined with "def" sentence?

We know that functions created with the lambda function can also be created with the "def" statement. What does this mean? This means nothing more than creating a function with either of these two statements is considered a correct action. This is because by both methods you can get the same result, with simpler options.

We can see this as a path, both reach the same destination, the difference is that one is longer and heavier and another is much simpler, as that is the lambda function used for, to make it easier to use functions in our code.

When we create a lambda type function, it will only focus on using a single line of code, thus minimizing the number of lines that can be used in a code, unlike the def statement, which usually occupies many times more than one line of code.

When using the lambda keyword, we create an object or function which is not going to have the need to be defined with a name, unlike the def statement which must be defined at the beginning of the program so that it can interpret it.

Although using the lambda function is much simpler for the code, many times the def statement is more understandable for those users who are starting as programmers and even for those users who have programming knowledge but not so much experience.

It is of fundamental need that at the moment of operating with the lambda function, this one is assigned a variable since if this is not done, the same one is going to operate only in the line in which it is going to be defined.

Chapter 6:
Object-Oriented
Programming-OOP

At this level, we are already able to design the program based on functions, so that we are able to use statements that manipulate the data. In this programming language, we can find procedure-oriented programming and object-oriented programming, which uses types defined by the programmer to organize both codes and data.

What is OOP and what are its advantages?

It is a form of programming used by modern languages, which consists of transferring the behavior that objects have in real life to the programming code. It is a way of organizing your program combining data and functionality by wrapping it in something called an object. Some of the programming languages that use this object-oriented paradigm are Python, C++, Java, Visual, etc.

As advantages we can mention the following:
- We can divide the programs into pieces, parts, modules or classes to this concept in programming are called modularization.

- It is a code that can be reusable, unlike what happens with procedure-oriented programming, so, if we get to create an application with this object-oriented program and later want to make another similar application we can reuse this code. Now in order to be able to reuse the code of one application in another, we have to know and understand the concept of "inheritance".

- If there is a fault in any line of code, the program continues to work, it is likely that the line of code that generated the error will not perform the intended task, but the rest of the program will.

- Encapsulation.

Object-oriented programming is responsible for applying programming techniques such as:

> a.   Abstraction: Abstraction refers to the process of design and interpretation, which focuses on recognizing the important characteristics of an object; thus filtering out and ignoring the particularities that will not be considered important.

Abstraction focuses on defining the characteristics of an object, which distinguish it from other types. It focuses on what it is, not what it does, and then specifies what it should be implemented in.

For example: We are going to apply abstraction to flowers.
Object: Flowers
Characteristics
- Colors
- Leaves
- Nectar
- Roots
Functionalities:
- Production of seeds and fruits
- Pollination
- Reproduction

> b.   Inheritance: some objects share the same properties and methods as other objects, and also add new properties and methods. We call this inheritance, a class that inherits from another, as happens in real life when in a family group one of the children inherits the skin color of one of the parents, he would be inheriting or having their own characteristics or

properties, but also one in common with one of their parents, the same happens in programming.

What does this mean? In a simpler way we can say that when we create a new class, we can implement the same data of the base class. This new class will have more specific data than the original class, which contains a more general view.

In Python, when a class does not inherit another, it must be inherited from an object, which is the main Python class that defines an object.

Once an object has been created, or once the class instance has been made, it is possible to access its method and properties and for that Python uses a very simple syntax which is, the name of the object, followed by the point and the property or the method to which you want to access.

Python also supports a limited form of multiple inheritances.

Types of inheritance:
-        Basic Inheritance: This occurs when a class inherits only one base class.
-        Multiple inheritance: This occurs when a class inherits two or more base classes.
-        Polymorphism: Refers to those different behaviors, which are associated with objects that are different, but may share the same name. When you call an object by its name (which has several objects), its behavior will be based on the object you are currently using.

Types of polymorphism:
-        Parametric   polymorphism: Parametric polymorphism is the one that allows functions and classes to be written in a generic way, in this way the data of the same can be manipulated without taking into account its type.

- Polymorphism of subtypes: The polymorphism of subtypes is the one in which the subtypes of a type (class) allow to substitute the behavior of the functions of the original type with an own implementation.
- Ad Hoc Polymorphism: Ad Hoc polymorphism refers to those functions, which vary their behavior according to the type of arguments they receive.

What is the terminology or vocabulary that we are going to use in OOP?

We will mention the most commonly used vocabulary to better understand this code:

- Class: Classes are models on which objects are built, that is, models where the common characteristics of a group of objects are written. To better understand this term we will do it by means of analogies, for example, if we have a car, the class would be the chassis and the wheels, since it is a common characteristic among the group of objects that are the cars. If we want to create a Python application that builds cars, the first thing we have to do is to create a class that defines what are the common characteristics of the cars we want to make and this class must have defined within it the construction of a chassis and the construction of four wheels.

In this case, to see another abstraction, let's show an example of classes, but in this case, the class will be a house.

```
class house():
    color="red"
    dors=6
    kitchen=True
    bathroom=3
    levels=2

house1=house()
print("We create a house")
```

As we can see in the example, the first thing to do is to declare that house is a class, using the reserved word class. Within it, it has some attributes, such as that the color is red, it has six doors, that it does have a kitchen, it has three bathrooms and two floors.

Now the next step is to create a variable and convert it as a class, for it, any name is placed and then the same is entered the name of the class and parentheses. As you can see in the example, house1 is an object, which has a house class and has all the attributes previously explained.

Finally, to know if the class has been created well, a print is made in the console to verify the proper functioning of the program.

- Exemplar of class, which is the same as to speak of the instance of class, and of object belonging to a class, which means that, exemplar, instance and object of class are synonyms; an instance would be an object or exemplar belonging to a class. For example, following with the automobile, we have already talked about that the class defines the characteristics that are common to it, and that define the objects that we are going to use, and we have seen that the class is formed in our example by the chassis and the wheels, but the objects that belong to that class could be different models of automobiles, that share a common characteristic that is to have the same chassis (it should be noted that there are cars that despite belonging to other brands are assembled with identical chassis) and four wheels, so we can have two cars with their own characteristics that are defined within the object itself (the car), such as color, model, weight, seats, steering wheel, then we could say that a specific car is an object belonging to the class, an exemplar of class or that is an instance of class; and another car of another brand would be another different object belonging to the same class, a different instance of the same class, or a different exemplar of the same class.

- Modularization; When we create a complex application applied to objects such as Python, for example, the most normal is that this application is composed of several classes, not a single class, which can also occur, but the normal is that if the application is complex it will be composed of several classes, the concept of modularization derives from an application can be composed of several classes, for example, applying it to real objects, if we imagine an old sound system, they were made up of several modules, the corresponding to the cassette, equalizer, radio, and disk, which means that the object was made up of several modules. These modules have the advantage to work in an independent way, that is to say, when the radio was damaged, we could use the module of cassette, in programming this leads to an advantage, if you have a program written in Python divided in modules and one of the classes for any reason fails the most probable thing is that the program continues working, just that the class in which you have problems will not be able to carry out its task as with the analogy of the sound equipment.

- Encapsulation; the functioning of a complete class of our object-oriented program is encapsulated, that means that the other classes do not handle any information about each other; going back to the analogy of the previous sound equipment, if we take the equalizer module of the sound equipment, the internal functioning of the equalizer corresponds only to the equalizer, meaning the functioning of the cassette module, nothing knows or understands the equalizer module, and that is what is known as encapsulation. Somehow all the classes are connected so that they function as equipment, but at the same time, each of the classes is encapsulated so that the internal functioning of that class is not accessible from outside. The different parts of a program are connected so that they form part of a team with something called access methods. Creating access methods we get to connect one class with another so that they work as a unit or a team, but these access methods will only have access to certain characteristics of each of the classes. You can access from one class to another so that they are connected to each other, but there are certain characteristics of each of the classes that are encapsulated so that they are not accessible

How do we build classes, objects, and how do we access the properties and characteristics of an object in Python?

To access the properties and characteristics of an object we use what is known as nomenclature of the point, commonly used in object-oriented programming, to explain what it is, we will do it based on an example.

Suppose that we have given our object a name, we call it myCar, all objects, instances or exemplars must have a name, in order to access the properties of the car in our program we use the nomenclature of the point:
E.g. Syntax: Name of the object. Property = New Value
   myCar.color="red"

This is the syntax in the case of Python that we have to follow if we want to access the property of the object, we use the nomenclature of the point. To access the behavior of the object from the code, we also use the nomenclature of the point.
E.g. Syntax: Object name.behavior
   myCar.starts()
   myCar.stops()
In the following example, you will learn how to access the attributes of a class, through the nomenclature of the point, so you can understand better.

```python
class house():
    color="red"
    doors=6
    kitchen=True
    bathroom=3
    levels=2

house1=house()
print("The house color is "+house1.color+", have "+str(house1.dors)+" doors")
print("The house have "+str(house1.levels)+" levels, and "+str(house1.bathroom)+" bathrooms")
```

The first thing we see in this example is the creation of the house class, which has its attributes, like the color, which in this case is red, the doors that have six, or the floors that have two.

Then, we can see how we create our house1 instance, which is of the house type. But we do not only want to stay with the creation of the class, but we also want to access the data that these have, therefore we will make a screen print of the attributes that the house has, as you can see, what we proceed to do, is to concatenate the string that we have written, and concatenate it with the attribute we want, now, to access to it, we have to name the instance, and through the nomenclature of the point, the attribute we want to access.

Now we are going to talk about how to build a code of what a class is; being the class the base to later be able to create objects, examplers or instances that belong to that class.

```
class.py       ×

1    class obj():
2            <statement 1>
3            .
4            .
5            .
6            .
7            .
8            <statement n>
9
10   a=obj()
11
```

This, more than an example, is an explanation of the syntax to the declaration of a class, because, although we sound repetitive, the declaration of them, is something fundamental in the programming oriented to objects, because as already you must suppose, it is the basis. Therefore, the first thing is to make the statement of the class nameobject():, with this, we are creating a class, which is named nameobject. Then, inside it, there is a cumulus of statements, which are responsible for giving value to the attributes of the instances and to work with the methods, which will be explained later.

There are cases in which you will ask yourself, but all the houses are red or all the plants have three leaves? And well, obviously the answer is no, for that we are going to work with the builders, they will allow us to give uniqueness to the instances. These are methods, but it is not too much to say since now that these are the ones that allow us to give different values to each instance, at the moment of initializing them, we will see them later.

Although you should already know what an attribute is, since we have worked with them previously in this chapter, we will now proceed to explain them formally.

Attribute:
We define attributes as those values that variables possess within each object. What do we mean by this? Let's imagine the case of a classroom in a school; an attribute that each classroom may possess is the grade the students are in or the age of them.

The word attribute can be used for anything after a point, for example, if we have the expression, z.real, real is an attribute of the object z, what we had previously called as the nomenclature of the point.

The attributes can be read-only, or write-only. In this last case, the assignment to attributes is possible. The attributes of a module can be written: module. the_answer = 42, these attributes can also be deleted when desired with the instruction del. As, for example: del module.the_answer, will eliminate the attribute the_answer of the object with module name.

```
class.py    ×

1    class house():
2        color="red"
3        dors=6
4        kitchen=True
5        bathroom=3
6        levels=2
7
8    house1=house()
9    house1.color="green"
10   print(house1.color)
11
```

The first thing we do in this example is the definition of the class house(), and within it, we define each attribute of the same, like color, bathroom, kitchen, among others.

The next step is the creation of the house1 instance, which is of the house type, as you may have expected, but if you want to paint the house, we will proceed to access the attribute, by means of the instruction house1.color = "green" in this way, the color has been changed from house1 to "green".
To make sure that the color has been changed correctly, a screen print of the color attribute of the house1 instance is made using the nomenclature of the dot.

Methods:

Since we have seen that each object has certain attributes that have certain specific behaviors; now we will call methods to each function created within each class. How is this? So let's go back to the last example of the classroom, it has two methods or actions which are to study and attend classes.

To create a method we use the word def, that we already know, but when we write it, there is a keyword that we cannot forget, which is a parameter of the method, this word is self, and this one is used to be able to access to the attributes of the class. We can observe that there is a difference between method and function and is that a method is a special function that belongs to the class being created, while a function does not belong to any class.

The characteristics of a method are the reserved word called def, name of the function, a default parameter called self.

Often, the first argument of the method is called self. this is nothing more than a convention; the name self means nothing to Python, in the sense that it is indifferent to put this as first or last parameter (because the position does not matter, but yes or yes it has to be the word self), but if you do not follow this convention your code could be less readable to other Python programmers.

If the concept of what attributes are, has been well understood, we will be able to observe that working with the methods is very simple, only that when working with them, we have to take into account that means to add behavior to objects, so that you can change attributes when accessing a method or return some value.

```
class.py    ×

1    class house():
2        color="red"
3        dors=6
4        kitchen=True
5        bathroom=3
6        levels=2
7
8        def open(self):
9            print("The door is open")
10    house1=house()
11    house1.color="White"
12    print(house1.color)
13    house1.open()
14
```

In this example, we see again, how to create the class house, but it differs from the others because it has created a different method, called open, as you can see, it makes use of the sentence def, then we will put the name of the method, then, within some parentheses, place the parameters, always, but always we must place the self as parameters, you can also add others, but the self can not miss. After this, it is treated as a normal function, as you can see, the method is responsible for sending a message, which communicates that the door is open.

Later you can see how to create the instance house1, which is class house, one of the actions that are done on house1, is to change the color of it, the new color is white, another important action is access to the methods, and as you can see, it is also done through the nomenclature of the dot.

Constructors:

Now that you have basic knowledge of classes, you should ask yourself if all the instances of one class are the same as the others, because if this were true, everything would be very monotonous, and the OOP would not be very powerful, as it really is, for this reason, the constructors have been created, which initialize the classes with values that the programmer wants.

A constructor, is the one that creates or assigns values to the initial attributes of an instance, and to do this, it is necessary to use a method, moreover, a constructor is a method of a class, to use it, we make use of the reserved word ___init___(self, a, b, c, ...), being a, b, c, the parameters that we want to initialize, since they are values that we can introduce as users and thus be able to assign the values to the attributes, in order to achieve diversity in our objects.

```python
class house():
    def __init__(self, color, dors, kitchen, bathroom, levels):
        self.color=color
        self.dors=dors
        self.kitchen=kitchen
        self.bathroom=bathroom
        self.levels=levels

    def open(self):
        print("The door is open")

    def paint(self, c):
        self.color=c
house1=house("blue", 5, True, 2, 1)
print(house1.color)
house1.paint("black")
print(house1.color)
house1.open()
```

In this example, we can already see how things change and become more fun, the first thing is that a constructor was used, the same has as parameters the self, color, doors, kitchen, among others. After the constructor's statement we use the word self and place the corresponding value, as you can see between lines three and seven, for example, in the instruction of line 3, what is said is that the variable color of

113

that specific instance, is going to have the value, what the argument has valued when the instance was initialized.

Then you can see how the open method was created, that method, only shows on screen that the door has been opened; the other method that has been created, in this case, is one called paint, which is responsible for changing the color of that instance, this was done using the sentence self.color, to specify that the instance is going to change.

Subsequently, the house1 instance is created, and it is given as argument "blue", 5, True, 2, 1 to the constructor so that he initializes his attributes in those specific values and thus to be able to remove the monotony that we had before.

After having created the instance, the color of the house is printed in screen, or well, better said, of the house1 instance, at this moment, it should print the string "blue", then, it makes use of the paint method, to change the color of the instance, to the black color, to verify that the color has been changed correctly, the color of the house1 instance is printed in screen, and for this case, the string "black" should appear in console.

Finally, the open method is used, so that it appears on the screen that the doors are open.
Since we know how to make use of the builders, we can apply the concept of inheritance previously applied, so that a class related to it, inherits, behaviors and attributes of its parent class.

```
class.py    ×

 1    class house():
 2        def __init__(self, color, dors, kitchen, bathroom, levels):
 3            self.color=color
 4            self.dors=dors
 5            self.kitchen=kitchen
 6            self.bathroom=bathroom
 7            self.levels=levels
 8
 9        def open(self):
10            print("The door is open")
11
12        def paint(self, c):
13            self.color=c
14    class apartment(house):
15        def __init__(self, color, dors, kitchen, bathroom, levels, stairs, elevator):
16            house.__init__(self, color, dors, kitchen, bathroom, levels)
17            self.stairs=stairs
18            self.elevator=elevator
19        def elevatoron(self):
20            if(self.elevator==True):
21                print("The elevator is in PB")
22            else:
23                print("You dont have elevator")
24    house1=house("blue", 5, True, 2, 1)
25    print(house1.color)
26    house1.paint("black")
27    print(house1.color)
28    house1.open()
29    apartment1=apartment("orange", 2, True, 2, 1, True, True)
30    apartment1.elevatoron()
31    apartment1.open()
```

In this example, we can see how inheritance works, since we have already seen the first lines of the code, it is not necessary to explain them in-depth, since what we do is create the house class, initialize the house constructor and create some methods such as paint and open.

Then, we define the second class, which is apartment. Why do we say that it is a daughter of house class? Well, we already know that an apartment is a house, but a house doesn't have to be an apartment, it can be a mansion or a townhouse, therefore it doesn't have to be an apartment, whereas in the opposite case, that is always true.

As we can see, at the moment of defining the apartment class, we enter as parameter, the parent class, in this case, house. Then we start the constructor, which should have the word reserved ___init___, and put the parameters self and all that those that are missing, with this we mean both the parameters

115

of entry of the class house, plus the additional ones of the class apartment, as it can be stairs, and elevator, since the apartments can have stairs or not, in an analogical way it is done with the elevators. They must be initialized as well. Later, as we can see, we will call the function of constructors of the parent class, so that the same ones are initialized, using the nomenclature of the dot, then, it is when the other attributes that are not in house, like stairs or elevator were initialized. A method that was created within the apartment class, was the elevatoron() which, depending on whether the instance created has an apartment or not, when calling this method, will appear on screen that the elevator is on the ground floor.

Already after having created all the classes, we proceed to create the instances, to verify that the classes were created correctly, in a similar way to how the object house1 was created, this one is created, with the same values of the previous example, the color of the object is printed, then the function paint() is used, and the color is changed to black, and finally the door is opened. Then, the other object that creates the apartment1, which has as arguments the orange color, two doors, True on kitchen, two baths, one floor, stairs and also has elevator. In the program is called the function elevatoron() to call the elevator and reach the ground floor, and show the user that this in PB, then proceeds to open the doors of the apartment with the help of the open method.

As we can see, object-oriented programming is extremely useful, since it allows us to see the problems of programming as problems of real-life and make solutions as if they were objects with which we run into in everyday life, for that reason, we strongly recommend programming this way, as it reduces the number of lines to use, and makes the code reusable, in addition to being more understandable.

Chapter 7:
Modules

The modules are files with extension .py (that we have been using until now), additionally a module instead of having extension py, it also has the extension .pyc; (what would be a compiled Python file), a module can also be a file written totally in C for those that are using CPython.

Modules have their own namespace, and in addition, they can contain variables, functions, classes and even contain other modules, a module within another or a submodule.

How useful are the modules?

The modules are mainly used to organize and reuse the code, this leads us to two terms that are fundamental in OOP as are modularization and reuse.

When we want to make a complex application and we need a code to reuse it since it was previously programmed in another application, this is one of the advantages that modules have, they allow us to reuse our code in different applications.
The modularization, in this case, we divide the module in codes, in small parts, when we realize a complex application, we can do it in a single file of thousands of lines of code, or we can divide it in small parts, in small files with a smaller number of lines of codes since it is always going to be easier for us to handle.

How can we create a module in Python?

We can easily create a module through the file extension .py, once created the file we can save it where we want, this is what we know as import.

Python provides us with a large number of modules in its standard library, in the official Python manual we can find this library through the following link: http://docs.python.org/modindex.html.

Inside a module, its name is available in the value of the global variable _name_.

Import Sentence

A module can contain executable statements and function definitions; with these statements, we are able to initialize the module. They are executed only the first time the module is in an import statement.

Modules can import other modules. It is actually usual to place all import declarations at the beginning of the module (or script, for that matter). The names of the imported modules will be placed in the global namespace of the importing module.

The import sentence has the following syntax
Once the interpreter finds the import statement, it will import the module if it is present in the search path, where a search path is nothing more than a list of directories that the interpreter searches for before importing a module.

Chapter 8:
File handling

The Python programming language allows us to work on two different levels when we refer to file systems and directories. One of them is through the module os, which facilitates us to work with the whole system of files and directories, at the level of the operating system itself.

The second level is the one that allows us to work with files, this is done by manipulating their reading and writing at the application level, and treating each file as an object.

In python as well as in any other language, the files are manipulated in three steps, first they are opened, then they are operated on or edited and finally they are closed.

What is a file?

A python file is a set of bytes, which are composed of a structure, and within this we find in the header, where all the data of the file is handled such as, for example, the name, size and type of file we are working with; the data is part of the body of the file, where the written content is handled by the editor and finally the end of the file, where we notify the code through this sentence that we reach the end of the file. In this way, we can describe the structure of a file.

The structure of the files is composed in the following way:

- File header: These are the data that the file will contain (name, size, type)
- File Data: This will be the body of the file and will have some content written by the programmer.
- End of file: This sentence is the one that will indicate that the file has reached its end.

Our file will look like this:

**Header of file
(name, size, type)**

_____

Body of file (data)

_____

End of file

How can I access a file?

There are two very basic ways to access a file, one is to use it as a text file, where you proceed line by line, the other is to treat it as a binary file, where you proceed byte by byte.

Now, to assign a variable a file type value, we will need to use the function open (), which will allow us to open a file.

Open() function

To open a file in Python, we have to use the open() function, since this will receive the name of the file and the way in which the file will be opened as parameters. If the file opening mode is not entered, it will open in the default way in a read-only file.

We must keep in mind that the operations to open the files are limited because it is not possible to read a file that was opened only for writing, you cannot write to a file which has been opened only for reading.

The open () function consists of two parameters:
- It is the path to the file we want to open.
- It is the mode in which we can open it.
Its syntax is as follows:

```
)                    🐍
1    function = open("file.txt", "w")
2    function.write()
3    function.close()
```

Of which the parameters:

File: This is an argument that provides the name of the file we want to access with the open() function, this is what will be the path of our file.
The argument file is considered a fundamental argument, since it is the main one (allowing us to open the file), unlike the rest of the arguments which can be optional and have values that are already predetermined.

Mode: The access modes are those that are in charge of defining the way in which the file is going to be opened (it could be for reading, writing, editing).

There are a variety of access modes, these are:

r	This is the default open mode. Opens the file for reading only
r+	This mode opens the file for its reading and writing
rb	This mode opens the file for reading only in a binary format
w	This mode opens the file for writing only. In case the file does not exist, this mode creates it
w+	This is similar to the w mode, but this allows the file to be read
wb	This mode is similar to the w mode, but this opens the file in a binary format
wb+	This mode is similar to the wb mode, but this allows the file to be read

a	This mode opens a file to be added. The file starts writing from the end
ab	This is similar to mode a, but opens the file in a binary format
a+	This mode is pretty much like the mode a, but allows us to read the file.

In summary, we have three letters, or three main modes: r,w and a. And two submodes, + and b.

In Python, there are two types of files: Text files and plain files. It is very important to specify in which format the file will be opened to avoid any error in our code.

Read a file:

There are three ways to read a file:
1. read([n])
2. readlines()
3. readline([n])

Surely at this point, we have the question of what is meant by the letter n enclosed in parentheses and square brackets? It's very simple, the letter n is going to notify the bytes that the file is going to read and interpret.

Read method ([ ])

```
1  myfile = open("D:\\pythonfile\\mypythonfile.txt","r")
2  myfile.read(9)
```

There we could see that inside the read() there is a number 9, which will tell Python that he has to read only the first nine letters of the file

Readline(n) Method

The readline method is the one that reads a line from the file, so that the read bytes can be returned in the form of a string. The readline method is not able to read more than one line of code, even if the byte n exceeds the line quantity.

Its syntax is very similar to the syntax of the read() method.

```
1   myfile = open("D:\\pythonfile\\mypythonfile.txt","r")
2   myfile.readline()
```

Readlines(n) Method

The readlines method is the one that reads all the lines of the file, so that the read bytes can be taken up again in the form of a string. Unlike the readline method, this one is able to read all the lines.

Like the read() method and readline() its syntax are very similar:

```
1   myfile = open("D:\\pythonfile\\mypythonfile.txt","r")
2   myfile.readlines()
```

Once we have opened a file, there are many types of information (attributes) we could get to know more about our files. These attributes are:

File.name: This is an attribute that will return the name of the file.

File.mode: This is an attribute that will return the accesses with which we have opened a file.

file.closed: This is an attribute that will return a "True" if the file we were working with is closed and if the file we were working with is still open, it will return a "False".

Close() function

The close function is the method by which any type of information that has been written in the memory of our program is eliminated, in order to proceed to close the file. But that is not the only way to close a file; we can also do it when we reassign an object from one file to another file.

The syntax of the close function is as follows:

What's a buffer?

We can define the buffer as a file which is given a temporary use in the ram memory; this will contain a fragment of data that composes the sequence of files in our operating system. We use buffers very often when we work with a file which we do not know the storage size.

It is important to keep in mind that, if the size of the file were to exceed the ram memory that our equipment has, its processing unit will not be able to execute the program and work correctly.

What is the size of a buffer for? The size of a buffer is the one that will indicate the available storage space while we use the file. Through the function: io.DEFAULT_BUFFER_SIZE the program will show us the size of our file in the platform in a predetermined way.

We can observe this in a clearer way:

```
1   import io
2       print("Default buffer size:"io.DEFAULT_BUFFER_SIZE)
3       file= open("Myfile.txt", mode= "r", buffering=6)
4       print(file.line_buffering)
5   file_contents=file.buffer
6   for line in file_contents
7       print(line)
```

Errors

In our files, we are going to find a string (of the optional type) which is going to specify the way in which we could handle the coding errors in our program.

Errors can only be used in txt mode files.
These are the following:

Ignore_errors()	This will avoid the comments with a wrong or unknown format
Strict_errors()	This is going to generate a subclass or UnicodeError in case that any mistake or fail comes out in our code file

Encoding

The string encoding is frequently used when we work with data storage and this is nothing more than the representation of the encoding of characters, whose system is based on bits and bytes as a representation of the same character.

This is expressed as follows:

```
1   string.encode(encoding="UTF-8", errors= "strict")
2
```

Newline

125

The Newline mode is the one that is going to control the functionalities of the new lines, which can be '\r', " ", none, '\n', and '\r\n'.

The newlines are universal and can be seen as a way of interpreting the text sequences of our code.

1.   The end-of-line sentence in Windows: "\r\n".
2.   The end-of-line sentence in Max Os: "\r".
3.   The end-of-line sentence in UNIX: "\n"

 On input: If the newline is of the None type, the universal newline mode is automatically activated.
Input lines can end in "\r", "\n" or "\r\n" and are automatically translated to "\n" before being returned by our program. If their respective legal parameters when coding are met, the entry of the lines will end only by the same given string and their final line will not be translated at the time of return.

On output: If the newline is of the None type, any type of character "\n" that has been written, will be translated to a line separator which we call "os.linesep".

If the newline is of the type " " no type of translator is going to be made, and in case the newline meets any value of which are considered the legal for the code, they will be automatically translated to the string.

Example of newline reading for " ".

```
1    string.encode(mode="r", newline= " ")
2
```

Example of newline reading for none:

```
1  string.encode(mode="w", newline= "none")
2
```

Manage files through the "os" module

The "os" module allows us to perform certain operations, these will depend on an operating system (actions such as starting a process, listing files in a folder, end process and others).

There are a variety of methods with the "os" module which allow us to manage files, these are:

os.makedirs()	This method of the "os" module will create a new file
os.path.getsize()	This method of the "os" module will show the size of a file in bytes.
os.remove(file_name)	This method of the "os" module will delete a file or the program
os.getcwd ()	This method of the "os" module will show us the actual directory from where we will be working
os.listdir()	This method of the "os" module will list all the content of any folder of our file
os.rename (current_new)	This method of the "os" module will rename a file
os.path.isdir()	This method of the "os" module will transfer the parameters of the program to a folder
os.chdir()	This method of the "os" module will change or update the direction of any folder or directory
os.path.isfile()	This method of the "os" module will transform a parameter into a file.

Xlsx files: xlsx files are those files in which you work with spreadsheets, how is this? Well, this is nothing more than working with programs like Excel. For example, if we have the windows operating system on our computer, we have the advantage that when working with this type of files, the weight of it will be much lighter than other types of files.

The xlsx type files are very useful when working with databases, statistics, calculations, numerical type data, graphics and even certain types of basic automation.

In this chapter we are going to learn to work the basic functionalities of this type of files, this includes creating files, opening files and modifying files.

To start this, first we will have to install the necessary library; we do this by executing the command "pip3 install openpyxl" in our Python terminal.

Once executed this command it is going to download and install the openpyxl module in our Python files, we can also look for documentation to get the necessary information about this module.

Create an xlsx file: To create a file with this module, let's use the openpyxl() Workbook() function.

```
from openpyxl import Workbook
def xlsxdoc():
    wb = Workbook()
    sheet = wb.active
    name = "test.xlsx"
    wb.save(name)
xlsxdoc()
```

This is the first step that we will do to manage the files of the type xlsx, we can see that first we have created the file

128

importing the function Workbook of the module openpyxl; followed by this to the variable wb we have assigned the function Workbook() with this we declare that this will be the document with which we are going to work (we create the object in the form of a worksheet in this format). Once this is done, we activate the object whose name is wb in order to assign it a name and finally save the file.

Add information to the file with this module: In order to add information to our file, we will need to use another type of functions that come included with the object, one of them is the append function.

```
1   from openpyxl import Workbook
2   def xlsxaoc():
3       wb = Workbook()
4       sheet = wb.active
5       sheet = ["B4"] = "Goodnight"
6       name = "test.xlsx"
7       wb.save(name)
8   xlsxdoc()
```

We can observe that this is similar to the last example that we needed to create a document, for it we did the usual steps: we created in the function xlsxdoc() the object wb, we activated the object and there we added the information. In this new space we will need to know the specific position in which we are going to write, in this case, we will write in the fourth box of the second row "B4" and these will be matched with a string that says "goodnight". The final steps are exactly the same as the last example, therefore, we will place the name and save it with the save command.

There is a simpler way to write and enter data, we can do this through the function append()

```
from openpyxl import Workbook
def xlsxdoc():
    wb = Workbook()
    sheet = wb.active
    messages = ("Hello" , "good morning", "goodnight" )
    sheet,append = (messages)
    name = "test.xlsx"
    wb.save(name)
xlsxdoc()
```

We can observe that we have created the document "test.xlsx" with the steps that we explained previously, we can observe that we have created a tuple called messages, this tuple has three items that are:

"Hello", "goodmorning", "goodnight".

Once the tuple is created, we use the append function, which will allow us to attach all the information contained in the tuple messages and finally save the document with the save function.

The append() function only admits iterable data, what does this mean? This refers to the data of type arrangements, tuples since, if they are not entered in this way, our program will return an error.

Read documents in xlsx

```python
from openpyxl import Workbook
name = "test.xlsx"
def xlsxdoc():
    wb = load_Workbook(name)
    sheet = wb.active
    file1 = sheet["C1"].value
    file2 = sheet["C2"].value
    file3 = sheet["C3"].value
    print(file1)
    print(file2)
    print(file3)
xlsxdoc()
```

Let's go back to our first example to get information from xlsx files, we could see that, for this, we imported the load_workbook class. The first thing we need to know is the name of the file we want to open and for this, we created the variable with the name.

It is important that the files are located in the same folder in which the program is stored, because otherwise the program will throw us an error. Inside the function xlsdoc() we will create the object wb that will be with which we are going to work, followed by this the object "sheet" is created which is going to represent the sheet that we are going to use.

Once all this is done, we are going to request the information of the specific boxes "C1", "C2", "C3" next to the function value, to validate that the information that we acquire is real, we print all the information requested.

Handling PDF files

It is known that the initials of this type of file are: "Portable Document Format", which have grown significantly over the years, are mostly used in business and education. This is due to the fact that they provide a great amount of benefits in which its security is highlighted, allowing to add access keys to control who can edit the document and even add a watermark to it to avoid plagiarism of information.

Other outstanding data is that these documents can be seen from any device since it is not necessary to have a specific program; in addition, the weight of the files is much lower since these texts are compressed, unlike Word documents.

A disadvantage of PDF files could be that they are not easy to edit once they have been created.

In this chapter, we will only learn how to create PDF files.

To create a PDF file the first thing we will have to do is to download the library through the command "Pip3 install fpdf", followed by this we can proceed to create our document:

```
1   from fodf import FPDF
2
3   pdfdoc = PDF()
4   pdfdoc.set_font('Times New Roman', 'B', 12)
5   pdfdoc.add_page()
6   pdfdoc.cell(12, 10, "First PDF program", 5, 6, "C")
7   pdfdoc.output("first PDF", 'F')
```

This is a simple level example, but at the same time, it is much more difficult than other types of files. To start a document you need a lot of commands, for it we will import the FPDF class from the fpdf library, followed by this we create the pdfdoc object and this will be the pdf document. Once created this document, we will have to customize the formats, size, and style of the letters we are going to use. To do this we use the command set_font.

In this case, the type of Font that we are going to use is going to be Times New Roman, with bold style and a size of 12.

Followed by this we will add a page through the command add_page(), since we will need a page on which to write and the function fpdf does not create a blank page by default. Then, we're going to insert information with the cell() function which contains a set of very important arguments.

The cell function will contain the width and height that the cell will occupy, it must include the message that will be written in string format, in case it is required that the edges to come with some detail included we must add 1 since the 0 is by default and does not allow anything to be inserted.

If you want to add a cell below or located to the right, you place a 0 and otherwise is placed 1, if you want the text to be centered to the right, left, up or down a string will be placed and if you want in it to be centered you write C

Finally, we will have to save the document through the command output(), and the arguments that will go with them will be the name of the file (with the ".pdf" included since we want a file in pdf) and then a string "F".

Managing BIN files

As we saw earlier, not all files are necessarily text files. These same ones can be processed by lines and even there exist certain files that when being processed, each byte contains a particular meaning for the program; for that reason, they need to be manipulated in their specific format.

A clear example of this are the files in Binary, to work with this type of files is no more than adding a b in the space of the parameter mode.

For example:

```
1   with open("pythonfile", "rb") as f:
2       byte = f.read(4)
3       while byte:
4           byte = f.read(4)
```

When we handle a binary file, it is very important to know the current position of the data we need in order to modify it. If you don't know the current position, the file.tell() function will indicate the number of bytes that have elapsed since we started the file.

In case you want to modify the current position in the file, we use the function file.seek(star, from) which will allow us to move a certain amount of bytes from start to finish.

Conclusion

Thank you for making it through to the end of *Python programming for beginners: The ultimate crash course to learn python computer language faster and easier,* we really hope that you found it informative and that you were able to approach all of the tools here provided that you needed to achieve your goals of learning Python programming language

Now that you have finished this book, you should be able to do a lot of programs for different situations. The next step is to keep practicing a lot, in order to become a master of Python. While programming, sometimes you might think that some things are impossible to code, or that you are not good enough to do them. But that is not right; you just have to think a lot in order to make it happen. Also while programming you may find that your code or program is not working, do not worry, even the smartest people write codes that do not work at the beginning. You just have to keep trying.

As you know, nowadays technology is everywhere and so programming is, our recommendation is that you try to code and solve problems of your daily activities in order to broaden your vision of the world since all electronics have hundreds and hundreds of lines of codes on it.

Good luck with programming!!

```
if: (you_have_doubts)
        print("Read_The_Book_Again")
else:
        print("GOODBYE")
```

CPSIA information can be obtained
at www.ICGtesting.com
Printed in the USA
BVHW062039010321
601387BV00007B/429

9 781801 792646